GRACE x 2

GRACE x 2

MULTIPLYING THE GRACE OF GOD IN YOUR MARRIAGE

ALAN D. WRIGHT

www.wyattpublishing.com
Mobile, Alabama

ISBN 13 TP: 978-0-9896119-5-4
Library of Congress Control Number:

Cover Design by Brent Piper
Interior design and typeset by Mark Wyatt

For information:
Sharing the Light Ministries
PO Box 5008
Winston-Salem, NC 27113
www.sharingthelight.org

Published by:
Wyatt House Publishing
www.wyattpublishing.com

For Bonnie and Graham

My parents-in-law whom I love

At first, I thanked God for your marriage
because it made me Anne.

As time went by, I thanked God for your marriage
because it made me a new family.

After all these years, I thank God for your marriage
because it has made me sure
that
love never fails.

Contents

Acknowledgments

My thanks to:

Anne. Love of my life, best friend for life, and co-heir of the grace of life. Your beauty and wisdom run deep. Thanks for multiplying the grace of God in me for 28 years.

Laura Hull. How'd I get an Executive Assistant who can run so smoothly an office, run so fast in triathlons and run so deep in the mysteries of God? Thanks for the untold hours of editing with such precision and discernment.

Executive Pastor Chris Lawson, Executive Director Mickey Thigpen and Executive Director Jeff Deaton. This book wouldn't exist if you weren't running everything better than I ever could.

The Sharing the Light team. Bob Roach, Marion Blackwell, Gloria Wommack, Daniel Britt, Stu Epperson, Jr., Dudley Hall, Scott Gerding, Jay Helvey. Thanks for sharing the light of Christ every day.

Reynolda Church staff and officers. Thanks for wanting to bless the nations with our message.

Reynolda Church. Thanks for your deep Gospel thirst that compels me to draw from only the deepest, purest well of Christ's love every week.

Mark Wyatt and Wyatt House Publishing. Thanks for your beautiful work and your partnership in the Gospel.

INTRODUCTION

GRACE FOR A CHANGE

Here are the three most hopeful words I know: *God loves you.*

Here are the three next most hopeful words I know: *You can change.*

For any hope of a deeply improved marriage, both statements are essential. And for any hope of real change, the order of the statements is crucial. But most people reverse the order of the statements believing that love is the reward for being a good person. *If I obey Mommy, she'll love me more. If I'm a star athlete, Dad will love me more. If I'm a more attractive wife, my husband will love me more. If I'm a more attentive husband, my wife will love me more. If I sin less, God will love me more.* So, craving more love, most people are constantly trying to change. But few succeed. Why? Because trying to change in order to receive more love is both wearisome and worrisome. It makes us

11

weary because we never know when we've done enough to be loved. It makes us worry because we're constantly afraid of losing the love we so need. Tragically, when we are weary and worried, we are at our worst. An emotionally exhausted and anxious spouse will be prone to all sorts of failures. In our efforts to "improve" our mates, we have too often unwittingly adopted the methodology of hell rather than the glorious plan of God.

Though it may be counterintuitive and contrary to everything we've been taught, people work harder and succeed more often when they already feel blessed rather than when they are trying to attain someone's blessing. We grow and flourish when we are convinced of our worth, not when we are trying to prove our value. We conquer our sins and correct our flaws when our acceptance is already guaranteed, not when we are striving to be accepted. In short, we will never become the people God made us to be until we embrace deep grace and break the bonds of legalism and fear.

Longing for a richer, more fulfilling and joyful marriage? These pages offer hope, inspiration, and timeless wisdom for your soul and for your relationship. We'll laugh together, weep together and experience the love of God together. But in the end, I aim to give you much more than daily inspiration for your marriage; I aim to show you a whole new way of living. Self-improvement manuals and marriage books might offer good advice and practical steps for changing things in your life, but that's not this book's purpose. This book isn't about how to change *things* in your marriage; it's about changing *the way* you change. These devotional pages don't offer *steps* to a great marriage – they offer a whole new *system* to live by. Build your marriage on grace rather than law, and you will release the power of God in your lives.

WHY LEGALISM WILL MAR YOUR MARRIAGE

"For sin shall not be your master, because you are not under law, but under grace." (Romans 6:14)

Bennett, our 19-year-old son, is an accomplished golfer. Throughout his years on the junior golf circuit, Bennett excelled with the putter. His putting prowess was boosted by a special gift he received years ago. Our dear friend, Bob Roach, wanted to invest in young Bennett's golfing by purchasing him a new putter.

"I'll take you to the golf store and get you that new putter you want. But," Bob added with a wry smile, "you'll have to prove that the new putter works. I want to see you make some six-footers on the store's artificial putting green. Make eight out of ten and that putter's yours."

The day arrived and we happily ventured to Golf Galaxy where Bennett located the precious putter.

"All right," Bob declared, "let's see how well you can putt with it."

Happy and blessed, young Bennett started making six-foot putts without a thought. One or two of the balls lipped out of the hole, but the boy was sinking most of them with the ease of a PGA tour champ. Suddenly, my friend interrupted Bennett's successful run.

"By my count," Bob said with sudden seriousness, "you're seven of nine. You have one putt left. Make this one or else."

What?! We had thought that the eight out of ten stipulation had been a playful joke. But suddenly, Bennett realized that the benefactor was serious. The eighty-percent-holed-putts requirement wasn't a whimsical ruse – it was a law. Miss the final putt and the putter goes back on the shelf. Feeling the pressure of performing under the law, Bennett did something absurd. He stepped out of his putting stance (from which he had made all those putts so easily), stood behind the ball and studied the line of the putt (as if conditions had mysteriously changed on the indoor green carpet). He hovered nervously over the ball. When he finally stroked the all-important putt, he yanked it left and missed the hole by a mile.

For seven out of nine putts, Bennett was at his best. But suddenly, for one key putt, he was at his worst. What changed?

In a sense, there were two boys in Golf Galaxy that day. Boy #1 was a carefree teenage golfer who was being blessed with a free putter. Boy #2 was a nervous wreck, worried about losing a free putter. Our dear friend, Bob, had already invested richly in Bennett's golf. Less than a year earlier, he had lavished Bennett with a Nike 3 Hybrid, a new 3 Wood and a Cobra Driver. The 70-something-year-old Bob had been a collegiate golfer himself and had played rounds with Bennett to help him learn and grow in the game. Bennett had only known grace and affection from Bob. Boy #1 knew he was blessed and highly favored. But as soon as the law was announced, Boy #2 appeared. He looked the same outwardly, but he was different on the inside. This Bennett was the same good kid and was the same good golfer, but he was no longer carefree. He was tense and locked up on the inside, worried about missing the putt. Boy #1, the one making the putts, had a smooth, free stroke and Boy #2, the one that missed his big putt, had a tight, awkward stroke. The law (making the putt) wasn't bad. Making the putt is a good thing – it's the desired end. Being honest, being a good husband, being a generous giver – they're good things, too. It's not a question of whether it's good to make more putts – made putts are good. It's not a question whether obeying God is good – of course it's better to be honest, faithful and upright. The question is how will we best accomplish the good that we want to do?

The story has a happy ending. Grace prevailed over law. After we laughed about how Bennett's putting would probably show up as a sermon illustration, Bob gave Bennett the putter anyway. The next week, Bennett played his best competitive golf ever, made more putts than ever, and received the runner-up trophy in the county junior golf tournament. But I kept thinking about those two boys: the Bennett who came to Golf Galaxy under a gift and the Bennett who crouched nervously under a law in the midst of the gift. My heart was gripped with the scene not for concern for Bennett—he knows he's loved. Nor was my heart concerned with Bob; he discovered long ago that it's more blessed to give than receive. My contemplation was about me and God. Which boy was I? The carefree boy making putts with a smooth stroke or the boy missing the big putt because of inward tension? And who was my God? A Giver spilling over with pure grace or a Giver Whose grace was tainted with a strain of law?

I had to admit that for too much of my life, I've been the inwardly nervous boy hovering over the putt he had to make in order to be blessed. I want to be a good husband. I want to be a good father. I want to be a good minister. I want to make a difference in the world. I want to succeed in all that God has called me to do and be. I just don't want the seeds of weariness and worry that seem to trail along with my attempts to be good. Too much of my life has been stained by tainted grace. Like most, I have been misled by a mixed gospel. It's not that I've missed grace altogether. Far from it! I've believed in grace from my earliest days with Christ. I've never been the child of harsh legalism. But I now realize, I'm the product of a tamer, more presentable grace and law mixture. *You're a sinner saved by grace, Alan. But be sure and confess your sin often so that you remember how much you need God's grace. Don't waste your life, Alan. There's a lot you need to do for God. You're going to be blessed Alan, but you need to learn how to live a godly life in order to appropriate those blessings.*

Living under the dark cloud of a gift with a law attached produces a terrible, gnawing, anxious feeling. If you are worried about the consequences of missing the putt, you're more likely to miss the putt. If your spouse is unconvinced of the love of God, he or she will be far less able to truly love you. The goal of any wise couple, therefore, is to get the law out of their marriage and the grace of God in. Multiply the grace of God in your marriage, and you'll multiply the intimacy and joy of your marriage.

WHEN LAW INFECTS GRACE

I am haunted by the narrative of a grown man recounting the childhood day his dad gave him his first fishing rod. It is a painful picture of a tainted gift. When grace and law mix, peace and angst also mix. His story started with the all too familiar tale of a distant dad:[1]

> *I now have no doubt that for most of my earliest days, the only times I was in any real contact with my father were when we fished together.*

Longing to be near his dad, the boy often followed his father to watch him set hunting traps in the woods. It's amazing what we'll do in hopes of finding a scrap of love.

> *As often as not, [my father] would ignore my being there and go on about his business of checking a set or running it again if it had been sprung. Other times, though, ... he would yank me to my feet and bring the switch across my legs. The switch would raise red welts that lasted for days.*

... I would make my way home and wonder why.

The law is most hellish when it is least defined. We, like the boy following his father in the forest, are too often left wondering, *Why am I sometimes beaten and sometimes not? Why won't she talk to me? I can't figure out what I am doing wrong. If someone would tell me why I am being   rejected, maybe I could fix it, but I haven't figured it out, and I am confused.*

One day his dad drove him to the hardware store where, as always, the boy stood by the glass cases and dreamt of new rods and reels and lures. When his father bought a new fishing rod, the over-excited youngster couldn't believe it was for him. But it was! The father gave it to his son on the boy's birthday.

> *I remember that day, though, when I saw him go into the shed where he kept his fishing tackle and came back with the new rod and reel and line. He just handed me the packages and said that he didn't expect to see any weeds in the garden that summer, that he expected to have the lawn mowed without having to remind me a dozen times, and that anything that comes easily could be taken away just as easily. I was almost afraid to accept the gifts because I never wanted them taken away.*

Sometimes a gift with strings attached is worse than no gift at all.

Imagine a single woman longing to be married. She's anxious about finding a husband. When the marriage comes, she rejoices greatly. Several years into the marriage she discovers that her husband is critical. He isn't satisfied with the way she orders the house, the way that she looks or the amount of money she makes. He sometimes threatens to leave her. She has the gift of a husband, but the strings attached are so painful that she wonders if she wasn't happier when she had no husband. A tiny seed of the law (*you must perform better for me to love you*) introduces an unlimited potential for fear.

Even a huge gift will become utterly tainted when the smallest of strings are attached. Imagine if I told my wife 99 days in a row, "I love you. I will never leave you. You are precious to me. I'll always be with you." And then, on the 100th day, imagine I told her, "I'm not sure you're good enough for me. If you don't improve, I might leave you." What would that one day of conditional love do? Wouldn't that single day cancel out all the other days? Even though 99 percent of the time I told her that I loved her unconditionally, that one percent poisoned it all. What would she be thinking about day by day? She would think, *Even if he loves me most of the time, his love could vanish without notice. I am not secure. I have reason to fear.* In other words, one percent of law introduces an unlimited measure of fear. Every "I love you" is tainted by the one "I might not love you." A gospel mixed with law isn't just ineffective – it's poisonous.

If you hear the preacher, or the Scripture or your own heart tell you 99 days in a row, "God loves you. He'll never leave you. You are precious to Him," and then, on the

100th day you hear: "You're a sinner and unless you clean up your act, God might not love you as much," the whole blessing of the Gospel will evaporate. A little leaven of law always permeates the whole loaf of grace. A million sermons about how God wants to fill you with His Spirit are rendered impotent by one sentence telling you how you need to get your heart cleaned up so God will be welcomed in your life. A gallon of beautiful, crystal clear mountain spring water mixed with a drop of cyanide is nothing more than a gallon of poison. Similarly, the power of the Gospel is in its purity. As soon as the Gospel of grace is mixed with even a drop of the law, it is no longer good news, and it no longer has power to transform us in a healthy way.

Because spouses want each other to be the best they can be, husbands and wives are always looking for ways to motivate one another. They assume that their mates will try harder if they are working for something that they really want to obtain. After all, it's good to set goals. We live in a world that rewards us for achieving goals. *If you make straight "A's" this semester, your parents will buy you a car. As soon as you lose ten pounds, you'll get that new outfit. If you can run a mile in less than five minutes, you'll make the team.* What do we want more than a new car, a new wardrobe or a spot on the team? Love and acceptance. We want to please the people whose love we need the most. We want our spouses to adore us. We'll work tirelessly for love and acceptance. Often without realizing it, husbands and wives convey a subtle message to one another: *I love you, but I'll love you more if you perform better.* Attached to this subtle message is an even scarier implication: *If you don't perform better, I'll love you less.* Thus our marriages, which were designed for grace, become driven by law. Sadly, our relationships often look like this:

> **I WANT LOVE**
>
> *What must I do to be more loved?*

> **I TRY TO KEEP THE LAW**
>
> *I'll try hard to please you. Am I doing enough?*

> **I AM AFRAID**
>
> *What happens if I don't do well enough?*

> **I FEEL BAD WHEN I FAIL YOU**
>
> *What do I need to do to make it up to you?*

YES, GRACE IS IMPORTANT, BUT...

Our first, natural response to the message of grace is: *Yes, grace is important, but don't we need the law? If we show others too much grace, people will take advantage of it. If I only show my husband grace and love, he'll take me for granted. If I don't put some conditions on the love I show to my wife, she'll never change.*

We've heard it over and over: "If you set your goals, apply yourself, and commit to being a good person then you can have a blessed life." Indeed, setting goals, applying yourself, and making good commitments are important. But according to the remarkable overarching story of the Bible, good goals, hard work and noble commitments aren't the source of blessedness, they are the product of it.

God created Adam and Eve, blessed them and then exhorted them to be fruitful and multiply. He didn't order them to be productive and promise to bless them in return. He blessed them before He commanded them. God affirmed Adam and Eve's value, demonstrated His affection for them and assured them of special standing in the world *before* He exhorted them to take dominion. Likewise, you will grow and flourish to the extent that you feel guaranteed that you are loved, blessed and secure. Every other form of motivation, like internal willpower, fear of punishment, or personal ambition will, in the end, not only fail, but will cause your soul harm. Law always introduces fear. Fear never leads us to life – fear leads us toward sin.

"Perfect love casts out fear" (1 John 4:18, NASV). The secret to intimacy in marriage is the absence of fear. The secret to fearlessness is perfect love. The secret to perfect love is the grace of God. Most people have heard the Gospel like this: *Commit your life to God. Give your time, your energy and your money for God, and God will really love and bless you.* It sounds so familiar that we assume it must be right. But it's all backward. The real Gospel is this: God loves you. He always has loved you. He will never stop loving you. Because of His love, God has blessed you in Christ beyond your wildest dreams. God's love for you is perfect. His love for you is in no way related to your love for Him or related to the merit of what you've done for Him. You can relax in His love. You can trust His love. Therefore, commit your life to God, confess your sins to God and serve God with all your heart.

THE NEGATIVE POWER CYCLE
OF THE LAW

LONGING FOR GOD

*How do I get
God's blessing?*

↓

LAW

*I promise to keep God's
commands.*

↓

FEAR

*I don't know if I've done
enough. What if I fail?*

↓

CONDEMNATION

I'll make it up by doing
more and being better.

THE POSITIVE POWER CYCLE
OF GRACE

> **LONGING FOR GOD**
> *How do I get
> God's blessing?*

> **LOVE**
> *God loves me perfectly.*

> **TRUST**
> *I'm valuable.
> I'm secure. I matter.*

> **COURAGE**
> I can make a difference
> in the world!

HOW UNMIXED GRACE HAS
CHANGED MY MARRIAGE

Shifting from a mixture of law and grace to a Gospel of unmixed grace has transformed my marriage in so many ways:

- When I am filled with the assurance of God's perfect love in Jesus Christ, I no longer look for my ultimate needs to be met by my wife. When I'm less needy, we're both happier.

- When I make mistakes, I am less likely to feel as if I'm stuck in a deep pit. I don't brood over my mistakes and, with less time in the pit, I spend more time on the journey of intimacy in my marriage.

- I don't feel condemned when I botch it as a husband, and I don't condemn Anne for her mistakes. The Gospel of grace has caused me to love the conviction of the Holy Spirit. Instead of seeing Him as a negative critic, I now view Him as the greatest teacher in the world.

- Without the tyranny of the law, I no longer consider myself a slave to sin, but I "count myself dead to sin" (Romans 6:11). This revelation has enabled a simple, powerful shift from thoughts like, "I'll always be a worrier" to "I don't have to worry." My old shame-based thinking kept me aware of my failings, but the Gospel of grace points me to the possibilities in Christ.

26

- I no longer see my sin and mistakes in marriage as violations of the law as much as violations of my identity and destiny in Christ. Instead of overcoming temptation by saying to myself, "God will not be pleased," I am more likely to say to myself, "Alan, you were made for more than this."

- I feel more confident in my prayer life. Together with Anne, I can approach the throne of grace much more boldly. I believe now, more than ever, that I really belong in the very presence of God. It's changing the way I pray for my wife and family. I pray bigger and braver.

- With no law threatening me, I see no doom over me. When my marriage is going through a rough spot, I don't think, "Oh no, I'm not blessed any more." I more deeply believe that I am blessed with every spiritual blessing in Christ. The more blessed I feel, the more joy and gratitude I have and the more love I show my wife.

- I spend less time worrying about what I need to do to be a good husband and more time thinking about how good God has been to me. When I meditate on God's promises to me instead of making promises to God about how good a husband I will be, my confidence grows. When my confidence grows, I'm a better husband.

In summary, the more we drink in the Gospel of grace,

the more we experience that grace multiplied in our marriage. When the grace of God fuels our marriage, we live by God's power rather than our own. God's way is always better.

ASKING THE RIGHT QUESTIONS

Whether they are looking to improve a good marriage or repair a fractured marriage, most couples ask me: "What do we need to do?" I know what they are asking. *What are the practical tools of communication we need to embrace? What can I do to get my spouse to quit being so irresponsible? How can we have a better sex life? What can I do to get my spouse to be more attentive to my needs?* I don't want to downplay the importance of such questions. Good communication, mutual respect, physical intimacy, and loving care are important in any marriage. It's not that these are unimportant questions – they're just not the most important questions.

It's more important to ask:

1) *Am I living under grace or under law?*
2) *Am I focused on my efforts to be like Jesus or on a vision of Who Jesus is and what He has done for me?*
3) *Am I motivated by my promises to God or His promises to me?*
4) *Have I accepted my new identity in Christ or do I condemn myself as if I were still under the law?*

Those are our questions for the next four weeks. There's a devotional for each day along with questions for reflection and discussion followed by a prayer. I encourage you to pick out a suitable time each day to discuss the questions with each other and pray the prayer for the day aloud. May you discover the love of God in rich, new ways and multiply the grace of God in your marriage.

WEEK ONE

Receiving Grace

Week One

Sunday

Grace Works

"For while we were still weak, at the right time Christ died for the ungodly."

Romans 5:6

I remember five years ago when I first attempted to put in writing my ideas about how grace changes us. I was at the beach writing about how the law arouses fear and therefore incites failure (sin). I had taken my first crack at the introductory chapter. My little girl, Abby, kept imploring me to play with her on the beach.

There you have the dilemma – I wanted to be a good dad, but I also wanted to do a good job on the start of the book. *Hmm.* I looked out the window. *The ocean is calm.*

33

The beach is uncrowded. My back is starting to get stiff. I'd like to go play. But no, I need a good ending to the chapter. Getting a clear conclusion is essential. Oh Abby, can't you see I'm working on this important book. I do want to go play but.... Then I had an idea. As it turned out, it was my best idea for the book thus far.

"Abby," I declared, "I'll go play with you under one condition."

"What Daddy?"

"I'll play with you on the beach if you'll listen to what I've written and tell me if it makes sense and what you think it means."

"Okay Daddy, but you promise you'll come on the beach then?"

I promised, read her a few pages, and queried the cute beach girl: "What do you think, Abby?"

"I like it Daddy. Let's go play."

"Wait, Abby, you promised to tell me what you think it all means."

Here was her eleven-year-old summary: "I think you're saying that the law makes you nervous and when you're nervous, you're more likely to mess up. But with grace, you're not so nervous and so you're more likely to do your best."

That's when I got up and went to play on the beach.

My friend and mentor, Dudley Hall, has written a timeless classic on the power of grace. It's full of rich biblical insights, personal anecdotes, and compelling truth about the true nature of the Gospel. It's on my everyone-should-read list. I like everything about the book, but the greatest thing about the book is its title: *Grace Works.*

It's a great title because it carries so many different meanings. It conveys the activity of grace. *Grace doesn't just sit there – grace moves us to action.* It conjures the idea of a factory, the *Grace Works.* But mostly, it captures the practical impact of the grace of God in our lives. It works for life. Grace works for the improvement of our marriages. Law doesn't work. Law never empowered anyone. Grace will empower everyone who will receive it. Abby was right: "... the law makes you nervous and when you're nervous, you're more likely to mess up. But ...." She might as well have concluded, "grace works."

For Further Reflection:

1) Read Romans 6:5-14.
2) Underline or write down all the words or phrases that speak of our victory over sin.

For Discussion Together:

1) To say that "grace works" is to say that shame and condemnation don't work. Share with your spouse about a time in your childhood when

someone tried to motivate you by condemning you or threatening you. How did it make you feel? Did it motivate you for the short term? Did it help transform you?

2) Share with one another a time that your spouse encouraged you by showing you grace. Let your mate know that "grace works!"

Prayer for the Day:

Lord, remind us today that grace works. Every time that we are tempted individually or together to use fear or shame to motivate, nudge us back to grace. Give us new eyes to see all the ways that Your grace has been at work in our lives. Grant us fresh vision of the fullness of Jesus' advocacy for us. Let us see first-hand how powerfully grace works as we share Your love with others. We pray in Jesus' name, AMEN.

Week One

Monday

Monkeys, Mothers and the Making of Trust

"For I am sure that neither death nor life, nor angels nor rulers, nor things present nor things to come, nor powers, nor height nor depth, nor anything else in all creation, will be able to separate us from the love of God in Christ Jesus our Lord."

Romans 8:38–39

Until mid-twentieth century, prevailing wisdom encouraged parents not to overly coddle their infants for fear that the children would become spoiled. But in the 1950's, psychologist Harry Harlow shook such ideologies with his famous, controversial experiments with Rhesus monkeys. In the classic study, Harlow showed that, given a choice, baby monkeys preferred a pretend, cloth mother that provided nothing but its soft feel to a stark, wire surrogate mother that provided milk but no "contact comfort." Both the wire mother baby monkeys and the cloth mother baby monkeys ate and gained weight, but the babies with wire mothers had trouble digesting the milk and were prone to diarrhea. When a baby monkey was separated from its cloth mother for three days, the infant Rhesus wasn't toughened up by its adventure in independence but instead became scared, insecure and clingy upon its return to "mother." The baby monkeys who only had wire surrogate mothers were generally insecure in unfamiliar surroundings and had little courage to explore.

Though some of his practices were criticized, Harlow's work was widely accepted as conclusive evidence that abundant parental affection was not likely to spoil the child but to strengthen the child. The more parental contact, the healthier the child. Interestingly, Harlow wasn't just criticized for the methods of his studies but was criticized for what he called them, "studies in the nature of love." It is not the withholding of love but the assurance of love that causes us to flourish. In fact, the more we feel guaranteed of deep affection, the more likely we are to become confident explorers and conquerors in life.

Such wisdom isn't new. It is as ancient as the Psalmist who cried out: "Thou didst make me trust when I was upon my mother's breasts" (Psalm 22:9, ASV). God could have designed you to come into the world as an independent, ready-to-go, self-starting contributor. But He didn't. He designed you to enter planet Earth as an utterly dependent, totally vulnerable baby who could produce nothing but some amazing diaper messes and some surprisingly loud shrieks in the middle of the night. You arrived onto this planet unable to do anything for anybody. In fact, you were a little bundle of needs. What did you have to give your parents when you were a baby? You couldn't entertain them by playing the piano. You couldn't impress them by making straight "A's." You couldn't take out the trash or wash the car or bring in a little extra income. It would be weeks before you could offer a legitimate smile. It would be months before you could crawl, say a cute word or take a first step. And having raised two children, I authoritatively can assert that it would be decades before you made your bed or brushed your teeth without your parents insisting so. It's God's design that we enter Earth with no ability to perform so that we can experience love, affection and care as unmerited gifts. Love, if it is to be love at all, must in no way be linked to performance.

For Further Reflection:

1) Read Romans 8:28 – 39 slowly.

2) Underline or write down every verb in the passage that describes how God has taken the initiative in loving you or that describes what God has done for you because of His love.

For Discussion Together:

1) Take a few moments to acknowledge and thank your spouse for some of the ways that he/she has loved you unconditionally.
2) In your own words, affirm your love to your mate without conditions. You might try language like: "I love you, not because of what you do for me but because of who you are. I love you just because I love you."

Prayer for the Day:
Father, You have loved us deeply, lavishly and unconditionally. May we love one another as You have loved us. As we begin this four-week journey, shed Your love abroad in our hearts. Reveal wondrous truths to us. Show us what a grace-filled home is like. Grant us grace to let go of any thoughts or behaviors that run contrary to the Good News of the Gospel of Jesus Christ. In Jesus' name, AMEN.

WEEK ONE

TUESDAY

Be Not Bewitched

*"O foolish Galatians! Who has bewitched you? ... Let me ask
you only this: Did you receive the Spirit by works of the law
or by hearing with faith?"*

Galatians 3:1-2

I met Jimmy and his fiancée at an outreach event our
church sponsored at a local homeless shelter. We served
free hotdogs to everyone. We offered free medical screen-
ings under one tent and offered to pray with others under
another. That's where I met Jimmy, at the prayer tent.

"I am so confused," his voice broke and he fought back
tears.

41

"What are you confused about, Jimmy?"

"We have so many different preachers come by here…. I don't know… something about 'God will sometimes take away what's most precious to you….'" Emotion overtook him and he couldn't finish.

"Pull up a chair and tell me about it, Jimmy."

"My father would never tell me that he loved me. I was working in a good job in an auto body shop. My dad always wanted to compare salaries with me. For a while, I was beating him, but then he got a promotion and started making more money than me. When I couldn't keep up, I decided to make money illegally. That's when everything fell apart and now I'm homeless. I've never been homeless before. I don't know where my dad is, and my mother died ten years ago. Do you think God took my mother from me because I was so bad?"

"Oh Jimmy, I'm so sorry about your mother. I don't know why she died, but it wasn't your fault. In this world, we all experience trouble. What happened?"

"Ten years ago, on my birthday, my father pulled into the garage and said, 'Brace yourself, your mother's got cancer. Happy Birthday.' That's all he said. That was my birthday present from my dad."

After we talked some more, I said simply, "Jimmy, there's a word for what you've experienced with your father. It's called shame. Sometimes, people who don't know a different way withhold their love and acceptance thinking it will motivate the other to try harder."

"That's it!" Jimmy exclaimed. "But no matter how

hard I tried, the acceptance was never there. No matter what I accomplished, the acceptance was always a little further removed from me."

I leaned in close to my new friend. "Jimmy, here's what I want you to know. God's not like that. In fact, God is just the opposite. When we were sinners, instead of withholding His love, God sent His Son to die for us. God loves us before we ever measure up, and God loves you, Jimmy."

I spoke gently with Jimmy about his father, but something inside me wanted to scream at the deceived dad: "Who has bewitched you? Do you really think that you are going to turn your son into something wonderful by telling him that he'll never measure up to you?! How foolish! You have been duped by the system of the world and the prince of darkness."

That's what Paul was saying to the Galatians. As soon as you start living by a system of measuring up to the law, you become utterly distracted from the purpose of life and the power of the Gospel. As Paul put it to the Galatians, you become "bewitched" (Galatians 3:1). Well-meaning people are entranced by a mixed gospel that adds law to the finished work of Christ. Don't be deceived. There is nothing that we can do to add to or take away from the love of the Father in Jesus Christ. If we want to see our mates soar, we must pour out love, not withhold it. Shame leads to fear and fear leads to sin. Be not bewitched by the allure of the law. Drink deeply of the grace of God.

For Further Reflection:

1) Read Galatians 2:19-3:9.
2) Paul was addressing the infiltration of the Judaizers amongst the Galatians. The Judaizers insisted that in order to be fully approved by God, Christians needed to keep certain Jewish laws like circumcision. Why do you think he used the word "bewitched" to describe what had happened to the Galatians?
3) Is there a part of you that is drawn toward rules rather than relationship?

For Discussion Together:

1) Did your parents tell you of their love or withhold it?
2) Share about a time when your parent showed you love through words, quality time, actions, touch or gifts. Share about a time when you wanted to be affirmed but weren't.

Prayer for the Day:
Lord, let us not be allured by even a little law. Let no one bewitch us with a mixed gospel. Keep the purity and power of the Good News of Jesus' all-sufficient work ever before us so that we will revel in the assurances of Your grace. For all

the ways that our parents have loved us, thank you. For all the ways that our parents have wounded us, heal us. But most of all, Lord, fill us with Your love again today so that we can love one another and others more richly. In Jesus' name, AMEN.

Week One

Wednesday

The Unfinished Sentence

" '...Now, lest he reach out his hand and take also of the Tree of Life and eat, and live forever—' therefore the LORD God sent him out from the garden of Eden to work the ground from which he was taken. He drove out the man, and at the east of the garden of Eden he placed the cherubim and a flaming sword that turned every way to guard the way to the Tree of Life."

Genesis 3:22-24

God stopped mid-sentence. The Hebrew grammar makes it clear. God couldn't, or wouldn't, finish His thought. I don't know of another such instance in Scripture.

"Now, lest he reach out his hand and take also of the Tree of Life and eat, and live forever—." God refused to finish the sentence because its concluding thought was an unbearable one. Instead of uttering the unutterable, the Creator moved to bold action. He drove out the creature made in His image and placed cherubim and a flaming sword to guard the path to the Tree of Life. When sin entered the world, so did curse and deathly consequence. But this hasty banishment and this heavenly guard were not part of the punishment; they were evidence of unending love.

There were two trees given names in the Garden of Eden: the Tree of the Knowledge of Good and Evil and the Tree of Life. One tree was forbidden, but Paradise wasn't smothered with prohibitions, it was dripping with permission. Eat and enjoy any of the fruit of any of the trees (including the Tree of Life). Just don't eat from the Tree of the Knowledge of Good and Evil. Remember the story? The Liar snaked his way into a conversation with Eve and lured her into the primal deception: you need to do something to make yourself more like God. How woefully ironic – the creature that was already like God (Eve) listened to a lecture from the creature who wasn't like God (the serpent) on how to be like God.

All dead religion is built on this basic deception: there is something that you need to do in order to be like God. That's the lie of the anti-Christ in a nutshell.

Eve fell for it, and Adam took the bait, too. Sin entered

the world. Shame filled the atmosphere. Curse and pain engulfed humanity. In utmost haste, God banned the man and woman from the Garden that enfolded the beautiful Tree of Life.

Why the radical exile and angelic sentinel? Why the unfinished sentence? Because the Tree of Life was the tree of eternity. The Tree of Life bore fruit for immortality. It was the tree that makes things last forever. If sinful Adam ate of the "forever" fruit, his guilt would become permanent. The unclean soul could not intermingle with the holy fruit without suffering eternal shame. God could not, would not, allow His beloved to be permanently separated from Him.

Instead, He removed the first Adam from the Garden so that He could bring the second Adam to a different garden. After sweating blood amongst the gnarled olive trees of Gethsemane, Jesus was nailed to the Tree of Knowledge. There on that cross, as the weight of the world's sin invaded His being, the Innocent One obtained the knowledge of evil. As He hung on that Tree, the east-facing veil in the Temple was torn apart and the golden cherubim atop the ark of the covenant were exposed. On that day, the cross became the Tree of Life to us who believe.

Fill your heart and your marriage with this glorious vision: you approach the eastern entrance of Eden to the Tree of Life, the cherubim see your spotless robes of righteousness which have been washed in the blood of Jesus. Instead of brandishing the swords of fire, the angels beckon you both, "Come. Have your fill of the Tree of Life."

For Further Reflection:

1) Read Genesis chapters 2 and 3.
2) Even in the Fall of humanity, God showed mercy. In addition to God's mercy in preventing Adam from making his condition of sin immortal, what other evidences of God's grace do you see in Genesis 2-3?

For Discussion Together:

1) The original temptation hasn't really changed. We're still tempted to think that we must do something to be like God. What are the ways you feel pulled toward that original temptation?
2) It looked as though God was punishing Adam and Eve by banishing them from the Tree of Life, but He was actually saving them from immortalizing their sinful condition. Have there been times when you thought God was punishing you only to later find out He was showing you mercy?

Prayer for the Day:
Lord, Your mercies are new every morning; how great is Your faithfulness. Even when we most deserve to be

punished, Your redemptive grace is at work in our lives. Thank You for the cross of Christ by which we have been welcomed into fellowship with You forever. Draw us into the garden of Your presence again today. Cause our hearts to delight in the fruit of the Tree of Life. Fill us with Your life so that today we can share that life with one another and others. In Jesus' name, AMEN.

Week One

Thursday

Backfire

"Then Nebuchadnezzar was filled with fury, and the expression of his face was changed against Shadrach, Meshach, and Abednego. He ordered the furnace heated seven times more than it was usually heated. And he ordered some of the mighty men of his army to bind Shadrach, Meshach, and Abednego, and to cast them into the burning fiery furnace. Then these men were bound in their cloaks, their tunics, their hats, and their other garments, and they were thrown into the burning fiery furnace. Because the king's order was urgent and the furnace overheated, the flame of the fire killed those men who took up Shadrach, Meshach, and Abednego."

Daniel 3:19-22

I love silly stories of criminals whose folly backfires on them. Here's one of my favorites. A District Attorney re-

quested the robbery victim to study the lineup of five people. The suspect was the last of the five in line. Each man
in the lineup was requested to step forward and say the
words: *"Give me all your money"* and *"I need some change
in quarters, nickels and dimes."* The first four spoke the
phrases correctly. But when it was the last man's turn to
recite, he stepped forward in frustration and blurted out:
"That isn't what I said!" Sometimes a bad guy's frustration
backfires on him! It happened to King Nebuchadnezzar.

When Meshach, Shadrach and Abednego refused to
worship the king's colossal idol, Nebuchadnezzar was furious.

"How dare anyone defy my official edict!" the king
fumed. "Turn up the heat in the furnace."

The more the men of God calmly refused, the more
furious the tyrant became. "Turn up the heat!"

"Yes, your royal stubbornness," the king's henchmen
replied. And they cranked the furnace up seven times
hotter than usual.

If the king had just left the fiery execution chamber
at its usual heat, all would have been fine. But because
Nebuchadnezzar was so hot under the collar, the pent-
up flames of the furnace backfired on him and killed his
"mighty men" instead of the "disobedient" Hebrews.

This idea of the enemy's plan backfiring on him isn't
new. It's as ancient as time. When the serpent slithered
into the Garden of Eden and allured the man and woman
into disobedience, the snake thought he'd won. But the
Lord declared prophetically, *"I will put enmity between*

you and the woman, and between your offspring and her offspring; he shall bruise your head, and you shall bruise his heel" (Genesis 3:15).

And so it was played out in a thousand dramas on history's stage. Joseph's brothers hated Joseph, sold him into slavery and lied to their father. The serpent had struck. But it backfired on the snake. God promoted Joseph to the throne so he could save the known world from famine and say to his brothers, "You meant it for evil, but God meant it for good."

Pharaoh got so angry he chased down the Israelites. But the chase of the enemy backfired, and the Red Sea swallowed up Pharaoh's army.

Five hundred years later, the enemy's taunts backfired again when Goliath's huge sword became the tool for God's man, David, to take the head off the Philistine giant.

And so the stories of the enemy's hatred backfiring on him continued through the corridors of time and the pages of God's Word until....

One day, Hell turned up the heat. Every demon must have been on assignment at Golgotha. The furnace of affliction could be no hotter. Jesus bled. Jesus breathed his last. The serpent had bitten. But on the third day, a new fire burst forth: the light of the glory of God. All the angels and all the demons realized that the enemy's plan had backfired on him once again.

If you are facing adversity in life or in marriage, pause today and consider how God is able to turn the enemy's plans back against him. Whatever your fiery furnace, don't despair. The plans of Hell will eventually backfire against the forces of evil.

For Further Reflection:

1) Read Romans 8:26-30.
2) Write down some ways that you've seen God take seemingly bad circumstances and turn them into something good.

For Discussion Together:

1) Share some of the ways that you've seen the adversities of life turn into spiritual triumphs for your marriage.
2) Share with one another anything in life right now that feels to you like a fiery furnace.

Prayer for the Day:
Lord, though the fires of adversity may grow hot, we praise You that You are with us. You have promised never to leave us. You'll never forsake us. Put our eyes upon Christ in the midst of trouble. We lay claim to Your word that You are at work right now to bring good out of all our circumstances. If the enemy turns up the heat, let it backfire against the forces of darkness. Let Your amazing grace bring us through, and let not our souls be singed. In Jesus' name, AMEN.

WEEK ONE

FRIDAY

No Worries

"... upon him was the chastisement that brought us peace..."
Isaiah 53:5

A wife bothered her husband every night of their seventeen years of married life crying out, "Honey, wake up! I think I hear a burglar in the house." Regularly, the dutiful husband stumbled downstairs, checked the empty house, returned to bed, and muttered, "No burglar." One night, however, the husband happened upon an actual thief in the night. As the burglar was trying to scramble out the door with the spoils, the husband announced,

"Wait, before you finish packing up our things, would you mind coming upstairs with me? There's someone in my bedroom who has been waiting seventeen years to meet you."

The real robber was *worry*. Any common bandit can take your belongings, but worry can make you become its belonging.

Most people think of worry as an unavoidable emotional response to life. We even applaud worriers as if worry is a gesture of love. *"I've been worried sick about you." "Oh, thank you, it means so much to know that you care."* Scripturally, worry is regarded as sin. Paul says don't be anxious about anything. Jesus not only says "don't worry" in the Sermon on the Mount, but in Luke 21:34, He warns: "Be careful, or your hearts will be weighed down with dissipation, drunkenness and the anxieties of life." He throws worry in right next to drunkenness!

Psychologists and scientists know that worry is terrible for us and any worrier knows there is nothing pleasing about the feeling of angst. Other sins have their fleeting pleasures. Lust feels exhilarating. Stealing gains goods. Lying protects or promotes. Even gossip puffs you up and bonds you with other mockers. But what pleasure is there in worry? Why would anyone *want* to worry?

Worry gives us the illusion of control. It seems irresponsible at best, terrifying at worst, to do nothing in the face of life's uncertainties. We want to do *something*. So we worry rather than admit that we have little control over life.

Under a covenant of Mosaic law, the people of God understood that blessing was contingent upon obedience. Disobedience earned chastisement. Under a mentality of works, our performance today affects our blessedness tomorrow. Knowing that we will inevitably disobey and fail, our souls are left with worry about the negative circumstances that might plague us tomorrow.

Jesus is the Prince of Peace, and Paul says Jesus, Himself, is our peace (Ephesians 2:14). Jesus is our peace not because He was a gentle teacher who calmed the hearts of the worried with His soothing words but because the punishment due us was laid upon Him. In the New Covenant, the only performance that matters is Jesus'. He made and kept the covenant for us and because we are in Him, we have been blessed with every spiritual blessing. Therefore, in the New Covenant the question is no longer: *What if I fail... what chastisement will happen?* For the Christian, the question is: *Because Jesus hasn't failed... what good thing will happen?* Everyone in Christ is invited into a revolutionary thought life. *Because Jesus took all the punishment for me, I can live in the peace of knowing that, at every turn, God is utterly for me. Instead of watching for the negative consequences due my sin, I can watch for the signs of unmerited favor every day of my life.*

If worry is putting a stranglehold on your marriage, try replacing the negative *what ifs* with the Gospel *what ifs*. As long as Jesus is for you, you have nothing to worry about.

For Further Reflection:

1) Read Matthew 6:25-34.
2) Why do you think people worry so much?
3) Write down your worries as a confession to God.

For Discussion Together:

1) Share at least one worry that keeps plaguing you.
2) Help your spouse to replace the negative *what if* with a Gospel *what if*. Fill in the sentence: *What if God blesses us in this way _____.*

Prayer for the Day:
Lord, You know how prone our hearts are to worry. We confess our worries to You and now, by Your grace, we release them to You. We cast our burdens upon You because You care for us. Thank You that Jesus has become our peace. Because He was obedient in our place and He died in our place, we ask that You silence the negative what ifs in our minds and fill our hearts with Gospel hope. Show us again today the glories of Your grace. In Jesus' name, AMEN.

Week One

Saturday

Bitterness Be Gone

"See to it that no one misses the grace of God and that no bitter root grows up to cause trouble and defile many. See that no one is sexually immoral, or is godless like Esau...."

Hebrews 12:15-16

We seldom buy new cars, but years ago we bought a new mini-van. The sunroof leaked, but the van ran well for years. When the odometer hit 99,990 miles, we piled our kids and in-laws into the van and rode around the neighborhood to watch it roll over 100,000 miles. We hip-hip-hoorayed like the hordes at Times Square welcoming the New Year.

We were celebrating grace.

When we bought the new van, we were issued a 36,000-mile warranty. We were entitled to 36,000 miles of a perfectly running automobile. But after 36,000 miles, we were on our own. Anything that broke from that point on would be our responsibility. I figured that every good mile after the warranty expired was a bonus mile. Or better put, grace.

When the writer of Hebrews comes to a big moment of warning in his epistle – the place where he's getting ready to shout: "WHATEVER YOU DO, DON'T BECOME LIKE THIS   SINNER" – he surprises me. In referencing Isaac's sons, I would have thought the Scripture would adjure us to make sure we never sin like Jacob. He was a liar, a conniver and a cheater. But the big warning isn't about avoiding a Jacob-like lifestyle, the big exhortation is: DON'T BE AN ESAU.

When Jacob stole Esau's blessing (Genesis 27), Esau became embittered and thought about killing Jacob. God seems to care more about someone taking offense than someone causing offense.

When Jesus warns us to pay more attention to the plank in our own eyes than the specks in others' eyes (Matthew 7:3), He's talking about the same thing. The worse sin is always bitterness.

What does all this have to do with 100,000 miles on our mini-van? Esau became embittered because he misunderstood his inheritance. He sold it as a youngster, assuming he was entitled to it no matter what he did. But by definition, an inheritance isn't an entitlement. An inheritance is a gift—one that you can't earn. Someone else earns it and gives it to you. Much of our bitterness results from an entitlement mentality in life. Entitlement thinking is like legalism – I pay so that you will fulfill your end of the contract and give me what I deserve. But all the good gifts of God are grace to us. Life is grace. Health is grace. Prosperity is grace. Relationships are grace. In other words, life isn't the 36,000 mile warranty that I've paid for. Life is free mileage on an old model. Married couples who live by grace rather than entitlement see life as a celebration, and when something doesn't go their way, instead of thinking about murdering Jacob (or yelling at their spouse), they grieve their loss and find comfort in the Holy Spirit (another act of grace).

I'm not saying that your spouse is an old model, but I am saying that he or she didn't come with a warranty. A great marriage isn't an entitlement. It's a gift. When you view your spouse as a gift rather than an entitlement, you'll be far less likely to grow bitter, and you'll be far more likely to be thankful everyday.

For Further Reflection:

1) Think on the words of Jesus: *"Judge not, and you will not be judged; condemn not, and you will not be condemned; forgive, and you will be forgiven;*

give, and it will be given to you. Good measure, pressed down, shaken together, running over, will be put into your lap. For with the measure you use it will be measured back to you" (Luke 6:37–38).

2) How does an entitlement mentality move into an attitude of judgmentalism?

3) Are there bitter roots in your heart? Bring them before the Lord.

For Discussion Together:

1) Tell your spouse how much you regard him or her as a gift. What are the ways your spouse is such a gift to you?

2) Have you been overly concerned about a speck in your spouse's eye? Apologize to one another for any seeds of bitterness that have sprouted in your heart.

Prayer for the Day:
Lord, let there be no bitter roots in our hearts toward each other or anyone else. Grant us the grace to forgive lavishly as You have forgiven us. Keep us from complaining of the specks in the other's eye and from the great plank of judgmentalism in our own eye. Let not our vision be obscured by an entitlement mentality. Fill our hearts with gratitude for the grace that You have shown us, and let us show that grace to others today. In Jesus' name, AMEN.

WEEK TWO

Seeing Jesus

WEEK TWO

SUNDAY

Satisfied

"... when I awake, I shall be satisfied, beholding your likeness."

Psalm 17:15

Marital bliss does not come through religious effort or any other activity. Sublime satisfaction comes through beholding Jesus.

Decades ago, when Mick Jagger pranced on the stage singing, "I tried, and I tried, and I tried -- I can't get no satisfaction," he touched something in the soul of a dissatisfied nation and the Rolling Stones became a rock music sensation. There's a link between our "trying" and our dissatisfaction. People today are no different than in

Jagger's day. People are tired of trying to do right, be right and get it right in order to find satisfaction. The satisfaction never comes. This explains why religion has driven so many people away from Jesus. Religious systems essentially tell people to try harder in order to find satisfaction. This probably explains why, when Jefferson Bethke posted a poem called "I Hate Religion, but Love Jesus" on YouTube in 2012 it received 10 million views in the first three days.

The vision of who Jesus is and what He has done brings bliss, courage and transformation, but the distractions of religion can strip us of the satisfaction we have in seeing Christ. Some years ago, our family enjoyed a delightful sabbatical wherein we traveled across the country. Part of the adventure brought us to the awe-inspiring Grand Canyon. We were there to see the Grand Canyon, but we planned some activities to "help" us see it. We planned a mule ride along the canyon rim. My wife was looking forward to the mule ride immensely. Imagine how dissatisfied we were when, upon checking in, we were told that the mule ride had been cancelled because a political figure was giving a speech along the rim of the canyon. We hiked down into the canyon, but I got winded. I was dissatisfied with my physical condition. Then a black cloud approached, and we had to leave the canyon. No one wants to get stuck in the Grand Canyon in a thunderstorm. I wasn't satisfied with the weather. Oh, and our room was small, and the kids' suitcases were in my way.

I was dissatisfied with my efforts to see the canyon.

But one thing is for sure, I wasn't dissatisfied with the Grand Canyon. No one visits the Grand Canyon and says, "Ehh, that's not so grand." No one says of his first sight of the Grand Canyon, "Rats, I thought it would be bigger." The grandeur of the vast geological marvel captures every soul with wonder. You can be dissatisfied with mule rides, rooms or rainstorms around the canyon, but you can't be dissatisfied with the Grand Canyon.

You will be dissatisfied with all the stuff of religion that often surrounds Jesus, but you will never be dissatisfied with the vision of Jesus Himself. He is altogether lovely and awesome. When you see Him you'll see that He is utterly for you and that His eyes are filled with relentless love for you.

There is no greater way to be satisfied in marriage than for both husband and wife to abandon all religious, moralistic efforts to be "good enough" and, instead, to become satisfied in Jesus. Here's the good news – just like the Grand Canyon, all it takes to be satisfied in Jesus is to see Him. Look to Jesus, both husband and wife, and let the grace of God be multiplied in your marriage.

For Further Reflection:

1) Read the story of the resurrected Jesus appearing to the disciples in John 20:19-21.
2) How did the disciples' vision of Jesus change them?

For Discussion Together:

1) What is the most beautiful or awe-inspiring sight you've ever seen?
2) How did the sight make you feel?
3) Is there an area of your life for which you've been seeking satisfaction in something other than Jesus. Explain.

Prayer for the Day:

Lord, grant us the spiritual eyes to see Jesus today. Let us see Him in Your Word. Let us see Him in one another. Let us see Him in creation. Let us see Him on the streets. Let us see the radiance of His countenance. Let us see the love in His eyes. Let us see the strength of His resolve to protect us. Let us see the joy of His heart. Lord, let us see Jesus today, and we will be satisfied. In Jesus' name we pray, AMEN.

WEEK TWO

MONDAY

Jesus, Our Hero

"When the Philistines saw that their hero was dead, they turned and ran. Then the men of Israel and Judah surged forward with a shout and pursued the Philistines to the entrance of Gath and to the gates of Ekron."

1 Samuel 17:51-52

Want more faith in your life and in your marriage? Learn to read all of Scripture through the lens of the grace of Christ. The Bible isn't an instruction book full of moralistic exhortations. It's one big story about what God has done to redeem us in Christ. When you read

Scripture stories as morals telling you how you ought to be a better person, you'll probably try to imitate Bible heroes like David. But even the most fervent vow to be brave like David offers no actual power to live a more victorious life. We're encouraged not by being told what we ought to do; we find courage when we see what Jesus has done for us.

I've been Goliath a thousand times and my boy, Bennett, has been David just as many. Though now Bennett is a bearded college freshman, in his younger years there was nothing he wanted to play-act more than the famous David and Goliath story. Toddler Bennett would swirl his blankie and release a wad of Kleenex or a dirty sock, striking me (the giant) and knocking me down. I was defeated countless times by little "David" who would race over and proudly place his victorious foot on my fallen chest.

Who doesn't love the story of David and Goliath?! The overlooked underdog runs to the battle line, faces his foe, removes the disgrace of Israel and decapitates the headship of the enemy camp. Preachers love the story. I've preached my fair share of sermons on 1 Samuel 17. Normally the application of David and Goliath sermons goes something like this: Be more like David. Follow his model and you, too, will be able to defeat your Goliaths. Preachers make good, solid points like: overlook the naysayers, don't try to wear someone else's armor, use the gifts (the smooth stones) that are at hand, don't look at the size of the enemy, remember that the battle belongs to the Lord, run toward your problems, don't retreat.

It'd be nice to be more like David. It'd be wonderful to put into practice all those principles in our daily lives. But telling me to be more like David doesn't empower me to be more like David. In fact, it can make me feel worse about myself. If I compare myself to the brave giant slayer, I realize how much I'm *not* like him.

If you want to multiply the grace of God in your marriage, read stories like David and Goliath differently. I'm not like David. I can't identify with a shepherd who risks his life for sheep, who is anointed king of a nation and who faces a warrior twice his size. You know whom I can identify with? I can relate to those cowardly Israeli soldiers who dressed up for battle every day but never fought. For forty days Goliath taunted them. They wanted to fight Goliath, but there was not one courageous man in the camp. There was no one righteous and faithful enough to represent them against the evil foe.

Have you ever noticed what happened after David killed the giant? The Philistines retreated, and the Israeli soldiers let out a giant, spontaneous war cry. Waahooo! Suddenly, the most cowardly army in the world became the most confident, brave battalion on the globe. They ran after the Philistines for ten miles, slaughtering them as they went and plundering their camp on their return.

They didn't gain faith by trying to become like David, their faith exploded by seeing what David had done. You don't find explosive faith by trying to be like Jesus, you explode with faith when you see what Jesus has accomplished. When you see the victory of Jesus over the evil one, you realize that you are on the winning side. You still have battles to fight, but you gain courage when you see Jesus. That's why Hebrews tells us that Jesus is the author and the finisher of our faith (Hebrews 12:2).

It's a good thing to want to have a more abundant marriage. It's a good thing to want to be a better spouse. But the courage and inspiration you need won't come by trying harder to be a giant slayer. The power for change in your life and in your marriage will come by beholding the eternal Giant Slayer, Jesus. Fix your eyes on the real Champion. See what Christ has done to defeat the Accuser and your bravery will soar.

For Further Reflection:

1) Read the whole story of David and Goliath in 1 Samuel 17.
2) Write down all the ways that David reminds you of the Son of David, Jesus.

For Discussion Together:

1) How have you generally viewed the Bible, as a rule book or a story about Jesus? Explain.
2) Is there a Goliath you're facing in your life or in your marriage? Reflect together about Christ's

victory on the cross as it relates to the Goliath you're facing.

Prayer for the Day:

Lord, You know the giants that we are facing in our lives and how prone we are to focus on the size and strength of the adversity before us. Help us today to set our eyes upon our Champion, Jesus. Give us a fresh revelation of the victory He won for us through the cross and resurrection. Turn our fears into faith. Move us from complacency into confidence. Let us see Jesus high and lifted up, having triumphed over the enemy so that we might take our rightful place of authority in the spiritual battles we face today. In Jesus' name, AMEN.

Week Two

Tuesday

Where is the Lamb?

"Abraham took the wood for the burnt offering and placed it on his son Isaac, and he himself carried the fire and the knife. As the two of them went on together, Isaac spoke up and said to his father Abraham, 'Father?'

'Yes, my son?', Abraham replied.

'The fire and wood are here,' Isaac said, 'but where is the lamb for the burnt offering?'

Abraham answered, 'God himself will provide the lamb for the burnt offering, my son.'"

Genesis 22:6-8

The Abraham and Isaac sacrifice story is one of the most perplexing, disturbing narratives imaginable. God tells Abraham to take his "one and only son, whom he loves" and sacrifice him at Mt. Moriah. Obediently, the patriarch takes Isaac, the son of promise, up the mount as described in Genesis 22.

In a scene of almost unbearable pathos, the father holds the knife above the boy's neck when, suddenly, an angel stays the execution and a ram appears in the thicket. Abraham calls the place "the Lord will provide" (Genesis 22:14).

I once looked at dozens of online sermons on this famous text. The application of most of the sermons goes something like this: *"Look at Abraham. See his faith and obedience? See his sacrifice? Let us be more like Abraham* (or in the worst cases *Why can't you be more like Abraham?*)". Then comes the questioning meant to convict: *"Are you willing to sacrifice for God? Are you willing to let go of whatever God calls you to let go?"* The implication is clear: *You aren't as blessed as Abraham because you haven't been willing to sacrifice like Abraham did.*

Really? Think about it. Child sacrifice was, according to Mosaic law, an abomination. The Canaanite pagans practiced child sacrifice and it was declared detestable by God. The Abraham and Isaac story isn't about Abraham's willingness to kill his son as much as it is about Abraham's confidence that God would provide the sacrifice. We tend to make this story (like we do other biblical stories) all about our sacrifice to God, when really the story is about God's sacrifice for us. The pivotal question of the story isn't, *what are you going to sacrifice for God (what will you do to prove that you are a good, religious person)?* The pivotal question of the text is "Where is the lamb?" The answer of the text is the announcement of the Gospel, "God will provide the lamb Himself."

We aren't supposed to identify with Abraham. We're like Isaac. We're the sons and daughters of great promise, born in a sinful world, justly deserving God's displeasure. Because of our human depravity, we deserved the cross. But at exactly the right time, God provided Himself as the Lamb instead. We're all Isaac, loved but deserving death. We're all Isaac, set free by a substitutionary sacrifice so that we can live out our destiny as heirs.

God provided the ram and then, instead of asking for a greater commitment from Abraham, God swore by Himself to bless Abraham. When you are in a difficult place in your marriage or in your life, don't ask: *What must I do so that God will bless me?* Instead, ask Isaac's question, *Where is the lamb?* Look to Jesus and ask: *How does the full, final provision of the cross of Jesus Christ fill my current dilemma with hope?*

For Further Reflection:

1) Read the whole story of Abraham and Isaac in Genesis 22.
2) What do you see in the story that reminds you of God the Father sacrificing His only begotten Son?

For Discussion Together:

1) Can you remember a time in your marriage that you faced a difficult situation and God provided a ram in the thicket? Share your thoughts and memories with each other.
2) Is there a challenge before you now? What does it mean to ask "where is the Lamb?"

Prayer for the Day:
Lord, You are Jehovah Jireh, the God Who provides. You have provided all we have needed in the past, and You will provide all we need in the future. Cause our hearts to be sensitive to the sound of the ram in the thicket. Teach our souls to expect Your provision. And, leaning not on our own sacrifice, turn our attention again today to Your all-sufficient sacrifice in Jesus Christ. In His name we pray, AMEN.

WEEK TWO

WEDNESDAY

Stephen's Miracle

"Now when they heard these things they were enraged, and they ground their teeth at [Stephen]. But he, full of the Holy Spirit, gazed into heaven and saw the glory of God, and Jesus standing at the right hand of God. And he said, 'Behold, I see the heavens opened, and the Son of Man standing at the right hand of God.' But they cried out with a loud voice and stopped their ears and rushed together at him. Then they cast him out of the city and stoned him. And the witnesses laid down their garments at the feet of a young man named Saul. And as they were stoning Stephen, he called out, 'Lord Jesus, receive my spirit.' And falling to his knees he cried out with a loud voice, 'Lord, do not hold this sin against them.' And when he had said this, he fell asleep."

Acts 7:54–60

The miracle of seeing Jesus releases us to experience another miracle: forgiving others. Classic preacher F.B. Meyer called forgiveness "the exclusive prerogative of Christianity… an exotic, which Christ brought with Him from Heaven."[2] Nothing is more essential to a growing marriage than forgiveness, but nothing is more humanly difficult than to forgive. Forgiving one another is not natural. It is not earthly. Because it is "an exotic," something foreign to all natural inclinations, forgiveness is only possible through supernatural vision. It is not until you see the One who forgave you that you can forgive your spouse.

Stephen was the first Deacon in the New Testament church. There are two words in the New Testament for the word "crown": the Greek word, *diadema*, which means "a royal crown" (from which we get the word "diadem") and the word *stephanos*, which means "victor's crown." Stephen's name prefigured what he would wear: the crown of the triumphant. But if you were there among the angry mob of religious leaders the day they stoned Stephen to death, you would have thought Stephen to be anything other than victorious.

Stephen wasn't given a real trial and the execution didn't follow the prescribed process for stoning a convicted criminal. Normally, the convicted criminal was placed in a twelve-foot ravine and was instantly rendered unconscious or killed by the executioner rolling a large bolder upon the convict. But Stephen's death came at the hands of an angry, impulsive lynch mob. The bitter crowd murdered Stephen slowly, rock by rock, bruise by bruise, cut by cut. The Jewish ruling council did nothing to stop it. In fact, one of the most vigilant, law-keeping Pharisees of the first century stood by overseeing the unjust execution. His name was Saul of Tarsus.

As Stephen suffered and died, he saw Jesus: "Behold, I see the heavens opened, and the Son of Man standing at the right hand of God" (Acts 7:56). Seeing Jesus took away his fear. Seeing Jesus carried him through the searing pain. But it was Stephen's final words that demonstrated the greatest miracle: "Lord, do not hold this sin against them" (v.60).

When a man is suffering death by stoning, no amount of Christian training will prompt him to forgive his executioners. When a man is being bludgeoned by religious hypocrites, he doesn't quickly check his wristband, ask himself, "What would Jesus do?" and then try to imitate Christ. Stephen spoke the prayer of forgiveness because he had a vision of the Forgiver. The vision of Jesus confirmed to Stephen that Christ is in control. The sight of the slain but resurrected Lord proved that mercy wins. Religious hypocrites had killed Jesus too, but Jesus was alive. When Stephen saw the living Messiah, he was flooded once again with the assurance that the love of God has triumphed. While the murderers hated Stephen, a vision of Christ empowered Stephen to love his killers. Jesus' ascended glory proves that love is greater than hate. Stephen was killed, but he was the victor that day.

I imagine that as Stephen fell to his knees, nearing

his death and crying, "Lord, do not hold this sin against them" that his eyes fell upon Saul. The Lord heard Stephen's prayer. Two chapters later in the book of Acts, the smug Pharisee Saul was walking on the road to Damascus when a blinding light shone upon him and he encountered Jesus. He became Paul the apostle who, more than anyone in history, has taught us the power of grace.

Whether you need to forgive one another for something great and weighty or something petty and light, you'll only find power to forgive when you behold Jesus, the risen One. Jesus' place at the right hand of the Father has proven once and for all that love wins. Hear again Stephen's invitation, "Behold…." "Look…." The One Who forgives wears the victor's crown.

For Further Reflection:

1) Read Acts 6:1-15.
2) Note all the descriptive words about Stephen.

For Discussion Together:

1) Counselor and author Leanne Payne regards forgiveness to be so important that she concludes: "forgiveness is the healing of memories."[3] Think of a painful memory in your life. How would

forgiveness help heal the wound?

2) Is there something painful lingering in your relationship because of a wound you caused? Take a moment to ask your spouse to forgive you.

Prayer for the Day:

Lord, grant us a vision of You today. Let us see You high and lifted up so that we will be assured that love has triumphed over hate. Without Your grace, we don't have the power to forgive, but by Your love we can let go of all our bitterness. Lord, help us forgive those who have hurt us. Help us forgive those who have betrayed, abandoned or wounded us. Keep our eyes set upon You today so that our hearts will be guarded from seeds of resentment. Lift our heads heavenward and keep us adorned with the victor's crown of love. In Jesus' name, AMEN.

WEEK TWO

THURSDAY

The Lens of Grace

"And now, little children, abide in him, so that when he appears we may have confidence and not shrink from him in shame at his coming."

1 John 2:28

There are two quite different ways of reading a verse like that.

It can be read through a lens of law: *Abide in Him. Read God's Word, pray without ceasing, keep fellowship with other Christians, meditate, obey His commands, and serve Him, so that when Christ returns, you won't be ashamed of how sub-standard your Christian walk is.* In other words, live a godly life so that when He comes again and sees how you're living, you won't have to hang your head in shame. Keep this concern close to your heart, constantly asking yourself, *Am I living 100% for Him? Am I doing enough? Am I witnessing and serving enough that I won't be embarrassed at my level of commitment when He returns?* By asking these questions and living with the uncertainty, you will keep yourself vigilant and train yourself to be a better Christian.

That's one way (and the most common way) of reading the verse. But when you interpret Scripture through the lens of grace, you'll see this verse quite differently: *Abide in Him, that is, read God's Word, pray without ceasing, keep fellowship with other Christians, meditate, obey His commands, and serve Him, because the more that you abide in Christ, the more your heart will be filled with a blessed assurance that you belong to Him. The more you abide in Him the more you will become confident that there is nothing whatsoever to fear about seeing Him face to face.* God wants you to revel in and enjoy the bliss of the inward certainty of His acceptance so that you will have abounding hope, filling your life with victory and purpose. The more that you abide in Him, the more your heart will be filled with Good News. The more your heart is filled with Good News, the less anxiety you will have. The more you abide in Christ, the more secure and confident you'll be. Secure, confident, Christ-centered people have little need for the sins of self-absorption and have much desire to love and serve God.

The first way of reading verse 28 arouses fear: *watch out, Jesus is coming back. Abide in Christ or else when He returns, you're going to be put to shame.* The second way of reading verse 28 builds faith*: abide in Christ so that you will be increasingly assured of how much He loves you and how deeply you have been blessed in Christ.*

One of the most wonderful decisions you could make for your marriage is to read Scripture together and talk about what God's Word means. But if you come to the Bible with a mental filter that turns every word into law, you won't leave your time in the Word with more faith, you'll leave with more fear. Law makes us resolve to try harder, but grace empowers us to live differently. Read the Bible together, but read the Scripture looking for the marvel of the Gospel of grace on every page.

For Further Reflection:

1) Look for the word "confidence" also in 1 John 3:21, 4:17 and 5:14.
2) What is the confidence that John wants you to have? How does that confidence change your life?

For Discussion Together:

1) How have you viewed the Bible throughout your life? Has reading Scripture been nourishing or guilt-inducing? Explain.
2) Share some words (either from Scripture or from your own heart) to build your spouse's confidence in God's love.

Prayer for the Day:

Lord, teach us to read the Bible with Your eyes. Teach us to see Your redemptive grace on every page of Your Word. We thank you for the finished work of Jesus on the cross by which we are assured of Your great love for us and given confidence that we are forgiven through His blood. Thank you for the gift of the Holy Spirit, a deposit within us guaranteeing our inheritance in the saints. Lift our lingering doubts and fears today by granting us new assurances of Your covenantal love. In Jesus' name, AMEN.

WEEK TWO

FRIDAY

No Fear Here

"By this is love perfected with us, so that we may have confidence for the day of judgment, because as he is so also are we in this world. There is no fear in love, but perfect love casts out fear"

1 John 4:17-18

Fear is poison to a marriage. When we are afraid and insecure, we have little capacity to love. Fear leads to hiding or lashing out. By healing our fears, the grace of Jesus enables us to overcome the insecurities that contaminate our conversations and cause so much covetousness.

In his Roosevelt biography, *Mornings on Horseback*,

David McCullough tells a funny story about a debilitating fear that Teddy faced as a child. When he was a boy, Teddy Roosevelt was afraid to set foot in church alone. When his mother, Mittie, asked Teddy about the phobia, the future president declared that he was terrified of something called "the Zeal." He explained to his mother that the Zeal was probably a dragon-like creature that lived in the shadows of the Madison Square Church sanctuary. Teddy knew about the Zeal because he had heard the pastor read about it. The wise mother got out the concordance and started reading aloud every passage in the Bible containing the word "zeal." When she got to John 2:17, Teddy shouted, "That's it!" The old King James Version rendered it: *"And his disciples remembered that it was written, 'The ZEAL of thine house hath eaten me up.'"*

Consciously or unconsciously, human beings have been afraid of God since the first sinners hid from the Lord in the garden. Fear of death and judgment haunts the human heart. The writer of Hebrews describes the defeat of Satan as a victory to *"deliver all those who through fear of death were subject to lifelong slavery"* (Hebrews 2:15).

Fear is an exact perversion of faith. If faith comes by hearing the Good News, fear comes by hearing the anti-gospel. Though there are many Scriptures that illustrate how the Gospel liberates us from fear, 1 John 4:17 will take your breath away.

"... as he is so also are we in this world." Linger there. As Jesus is now in the Heavenlies, so are we in this world. How can we already be like Jesus? He's God, we're not. He

never sinned, we've fallen many times. He's the Creator, we're creatures. How can John say we are "as He is"?

Here's the breathtaking truth: when you accept Christ, you are declared innocent. You are as guiltless as Jesus. There's more. When you accept Christ, you are imputed with Jesus' righteousness. Though it staggers our minds, it means that we are reckoned by God to be just as good as Jesus.

God loves you just as much as He loves Jesus.

He loves you perfectly. Meditate on His perfect love for you, and it will cast out all your fears. Cast out your fears and you get rid of your insecurity and neediness. Get rid of your insecurities and you have much more love to give your mate.

What little Teddy didn't know was that when the zeal of the Lord eats you up, you aren't filled with fear, you're filled with faith! If you want to help your spouse and help your marriage, you'll do a lot more good by building faith than by arousing fear. Let the love of God fill your hearts so that all fear will be cast out of your marriage. Then, and only then, will marriage be as God designed.

For Further Reflection:

1) Think about theologian Wayne Grudem's words: "When we say that God imputes Christ's righteousness to us it means that God thinks of

Christ's righteousness as belonging to us, or re-gards it as belonging to us."[4]

2) Is it easier to believe that you are forgiven than it is to believe that you are reckoned as the righteousness of Christ? Why?

For Discussion Together:

1) Share one of your fears with your spouse.
2) How can the perfect love of God alleviate that fear?

Prayer for the Day:

Lord, we give You praise and honor and glory this day. By Your Son's blood, You have forgiven us, set us free and declared us to be the righteousness of Christ. We have no merit to deserve such lavish grace, but we embrace our new position in Christ. Convince our hearts that we are fully adopted, heirs with Christ, and perfectly loved by You so that our fears will be dissolved, and we will be free to love one another more deeply. In Jesus' name, AMEN.

WEEK TWO

SATURDAY

Follow Me

"As Jesus passed on from there, he saw a man called Matthew sitting at the tax booth, and he said to him, 'Follow me!' And he rose and followed him."

Matthew 9:9

Marriage is God's gift of deepest intimacy for two people who are called to Jesus before they are called to each other. When you and your spouse follow Christ more closely you become closer to each other.

According to a CBS News report of a study on the increasing social isolation in America, from 1985 to 2004, "the number of people saying there is no one with whom they discuss important matters nearly tripled." In this new millennium, 24.6 percent of people report they have no confidants, either family or non-family. One in four Americans do not have one person in whom they can confide? It gets worse. Another 19.6 percent of people say they have just one confidant. That means 44 percent of Americans have either no confidants or just one.[5]

People aren't just lonely. They are being stripped of their deepest longing – to know and be known.

No one seems to know for sure what's causing this slide into isolationism. Surprisingly, it's not the Internet and social media. Most sociologists think the decline is more related to the automobile commute and to the television. Whatever may be the cause, the effect is the same. We couldn't have fallen into a more subtle or threatening trap set by the enemy. We are made for relationship and impoverished without intimacy. Without close, meaningful fellowship, we will be forever void of the joy and inward strength that makes us move into the world with purpose. We will settle for all manner of superficial substitutes for real relationship.

It is into this relationship-starved America that the Gospel extends the astounding command of Jesus: "Follow me." It is, like all of Jesus' commands, astonishing good news. When Jesus invites you to follow Him, it means that you are invited to be close to Him.

"Follow me" was Jesus' invitation to one of the most despised men in Jewish society – Matthew, the tax collector. Tax collectors were despised because they were viewed as traitors. They worked for Rome while robbing their own countrymen. Matthew had no real friends in the Roman government and no real friends in the Hebrew culture. He grew filthy rich and could feel the pulse of power while he sat at his tax booth, but he was bankrupt of human relationship.

It is to the Matthew in all of us that Jesus says: "Follow me."

His invitation to discipleship is an invitation to intimacy. When you hear Jesus say, "Follow me", you are hearing the Lord of the Universe invite you into His inner circle. When He invited Matthew into that circle, it wasn't for a "me and Jesus" Christianity, it was to be with Jesus and eleven other unlikely disciples. The Christian Gospel is the answer to culture's emptiness in manifold ways, but perhaps in no greater way than this: we come to life through relationship. When both husband and wife hear Jesus say "Follow me" and say "Yes, thank you," the man and woman find intimacy with one another because of their intimacy with Jesus.

Hear Christ beckon you today. "I love you. I died for you. I intercede for you. Come, follow me."

For Further Reflection:

1) Read Matthew 9:9-13.
2) How does Jesus' statement "those who are well

have no need of a physician" clarify what He means when He tells Matthew "Follow me"?

3) When you hear Jesus say, "Follow me", does it feel like good news or a hard command?

For Discussion Together:

1) Share about a time when you felt lonely.
2) When do you feel closest to your spouse? Explain.
3) Share with your spouse your favorite way of spending time together.

Prayer for the Day:

Lord, thank You that You came to us while we were still in our sin. Thank You that You called us to follow You though we didn't deserve to be with You. Speak again to the deepest places in our heart and beckon us close to Your side. Draw us close to Your heart. Give us ears to hear Your call, eyes to see where You are leading and hearts glad to follow You. Make our relationship closer by bringing us closer to You. In Jesus' name, AMEN.

WEEK THREE

Trusting God's Promises

WEEK THREE

SUNDAY

Your Place in the Palace

"And David said, 'Is there still anyone left of the house of Saul, that I may show him kindness for Jonathan's sake?'"

2 Samuel 9:1

The Old Covenant was a covenant between God and the people. God made His promises and the people pledged their oath to obey. If the people obeyed, they would be blessed. But no matter how hard they tried and how good their intentions were, the people kept disobeying. The New Covenant, on the other hand, wasn't between God and the people. It was between God and one person, Jesus. Jesus represented us in the covenant. The New Covenant is between the Father and the Son. The Father promised to bless humanity, and the Son promised to never disobey the Father, all the way to the cross of Calvary. The Son made and kept the covenant on our behalf so that anyone who believes in Him is *in Christ*. The reason we are "blessed with every spiritual blessing" is because we were "chosen in him" (Ephesians 1:3-4). The reason you have a seat at God's royal banquet table is because a covenant was made and kept for you; your place at the table has nothing to do with your own righteousness. The joy and power of the Christian's life is built upon God's promises to us rather than our vows to God.

Mephibosheth's name means shame. He was disabled by a childhood accident and hid in obscurity for most of his life. It seemed he was forgotten and useless. What Mephibosheth couldn't foresee was that a covenant would be made and kept on his behalf. Mephibosheth's father, Jonathon, loved a soon-to-be-king named David, but Jonathon's father, King Saul, jealously tried to kill David. As Saul's dethronement neared, Jonathon made a covenant with David. Jonathon would do all he could to protect David from the murderous Saul and Jonathon asked David: *"If I am still alive, show me the steadfast love of the LORD, that I may not die; and do not cut off your steadfast love from my house forever, when the LORD cuts off every one of the enemies of David from the face of the earth"* (1 Samuel 20:14–15). The covenant was clear. Jonathon pledged to protect and bless David. David pledged to show love to all of Jonathon's descendants.

One day, after Saul and Jonathon had been killed and

David had become king of Israel, King David remembered his covenant with Jonathon and asked: *"Is there still any-one left of the house of Saul, that I may show him kind-ness for Jonathan's sake?"* (2 Samuel 9:1). David's servant Ziba reported that there was one descendant of Jonathon living. So David sent for Jonathon's crippled, fearful son, Mephibosheth. Note this well and seal it upon your heart. The king didn't send for Mephibosheth because of any virtue within Mephibosheth. The king's covenant was with Jonathon. Mephibosheth benefited from a covenant he didn't make. Mephibosheth was blessed because he was *in Jonathon*.

Mephibosheth must have assumed the king's troops had found him in order to execute him. That's what most new kings would do - eliminate potential threats to the throne. The trembling, crippled son of Jonathon cowered before King David who stunned Mephibosheth with his words: "Do not fear, for I will show you kindness for the sake of your father Jonathon..." (v.7).

Mephibosheth stammered in disbelief: "What is your servant, that you should show regard for a dead dog such as I?" (v.8). It was hard for him to believe that he would be blessed when he expected to be killed. It was hard for him to believe that the king would bless him when he hadn't done anything to deserve it. David declared simply: "Me-phibosheth ... shall always eat at my table" (v.10).

As surely as Mephibosheth gained a place in the pal-ace by no merit of his own, you have been given a place at the King's table by no righteousness of your own. You are blessed with every spiritual blessing simply because you are "in Christ." Christ made and kept a covenant with the Father on your behalf. The Father pours out His blessings upon you not because you deserve such lavish grace, but because the Father promised to bless you through His Son. Don't build your life and your marriage on your efforts or vows to God, but on God's covenant vows to you in Christ. No matter what has shamed or crippled you in the past, take your seat today at the royal banquet table. You didn't earn it or deserve it, but you have a place in the palace forever.

For Further Reflection:

1) Read 1 Samuel 20:1-17, 2 Samuel 4:4, and 2 Samuel 9:1-13 for the whole story of David, Jonathon and Mephibosheth.

2) What do you think Mephibosheth's life was like before David invited him to the palace? What do you think it was like for Mephibosheth the first time he ate at the king's table?

For Discussion Together:

1) Was there ever a time in which you were given an honor or award that you felt you didn't deserve?

What was that experience like?

2) Do you see your life as a Christian more like Mephibosheth in hiding or Mephibosheth in the palace? Explain.

Prayer for the Day:

Lord, show us the wonders of the New Covenant that was made and kept in Christ Jesus. Your grace and kindness to us is greater than our minds can comprehend. We deserve punishment, but instead we have been blessed with every spiritual blessing in Christ. Cause our hearts to welcome such lavish grace, and teach us what it means to live by Your promises to us rather than our promises to You. Build our faith today by reminding us of Mephibosheth who was afraid and undeserving but who ate at the king's table. Keep us aware of our place in Your palace through the New Covenant of grace. In Jesus' name, AMEN.

WEEK THREE

MONDAY

The Birthplace of Unbiblical Oaths

"Now the LORD said to Abram, 'Go from your country and your kindred and your father's house to the land that I will show you. And I will make of you a great nation, and I will bless you and make your name great, so that you will be a blessing. I will bless those who bless you, and him who dishonors you I will curse, and in you all the families of the earth shall be blessed.'"

Genesis 12:1-3

Ruth Graham was once asked if she had ever considered divorcing her famed evangelist husband, Billy. In her unique wit, Ruth replied: "Divorce? Never. Murder? Yes." Vows confirm that you are married in the eyes of the state, but they don't equip you to love. Anyone who has tasted the pain of abandonment, unfaithfulness or divorce knows that vows don't guarantee affection. Love comes from God, not from vows. In fact, most of us harbor unconscious, ungodly vows that enslave us. The abundant Christian life isn't fueled by our promises to God – it is inspired by God's promises to us.

When life hurts, we'll do just about anything to avoid feeling the pain. Life hurt me when I was ten years old, and I saw my dad cry for the first time. He said he felt like a failure, that he and Mom had problems, and that he was leaving home. That family meeting ransacked my heart and my fourth grade world.

I never said it out loud. I never wrote it on a piece of paper. I never rehearsed it in my head. But I made a secret oath the day my dad left. *I'll never rest until I have my family back together, happy and healthy again.*

I was a hurting, confused fourth grade boy. I didn't know why Dad was leaving, but surely there was something that would compel my father homeward. Too ashamed to talk to anyone about it and too much of a big boy to cry in someone's arms, all I knew to do was to try to get my family back together. It was the only way I knew to deal with my pain. But what's a ten-year-old boy to do in order to win his father's return home? *I could do even better at school. I could do more than make straight "A's" – I could try to make a perfect score on every test! Or maybe I could be the best tennis player ever. First, I'll win the city tournament and then I'll be the best player in High School.*

Did I really, consciously think, "If I'm a perfect student and remarkable athlete then my father will reconcile with my mother?" No, even to a fourth grader, that would seem absurd. But it's not the vows that we're conscious of that rule us. We're actually more driven by our silent, unconscious oaths.

Ramping up our vows to be better spouses will never make our marriages flourish. They will flourish when we embrace the vows of God to us. It is ultimately the promise of God to me – that He will never leave me nor forsake me, that makes me secure enough to never leave nor forsake my wife. Build your life on God's vows to you rather than on your vows to God.

For Further Reflection:

1) Re-read today's Scripture, Genesis 12: 1-3. What are God's promises to Abraham?
2) Abraham is highlighted in Scripture as a picture of faith. Do you find it surprising that Abraham doesn't make vows to God?

For Discussion Together:

1) Have you ever made a vow to God? Share it with your spouse. Has the vow empowered you or enslaved you?

2) Think of three promises that God has made to you in His Word. Speak those promises personally over one another.

Prayer for the Day:
Lord, expose all our hidden, ungodly oaths so that we will not be driven by self-made rules. We have been set free and forgiven by what You have done for us not by what we have done for You. Let Your grace, not our vows be the fuel for victorious living and an abundant marriage. Remind us throughout the day of Your promises to us so that our faith will grow and You will be exalted in us. In Jesus' name, AMEN.

WEEK THREE

TUESDAY

The Dangers of Unbiblical Oaths

"The sting of death is sin, and the power of sin is the law. But thanks be to God, who gives us the victory through our Lord Jesus Christ."

1 Corinthians 15:56–57

John and Paula Sandford, pioneers in the ministry of emotional healing, discovered through their counseling practice the destructive power that ungodly inner vows can have. A woman came to them who longed to bear a male child but had suffered tragic pregnancies. Several times she miscarried unborn boys at the end of her first trimester. Physicians diagnosed no medical reason for the miscarriages. During the young woman's counseling with the Sandfords, she shared how cruelly her older brother had treated her during her childhood. He was a vicious brother, belittling her and physically abusing her. During a counseling session, the woman remembered a scene from her childhood. She was a nine-year-old girl, walking beside a river, picking up stones, and as she threw them in the water, she was crying out: "I'll never carry a boy child. I'll never carry a boy child." The memory revealed that her adult longings were in conflict with her childhood vows. After the Sandfords prayed with her, and she forgave her brother, the woman was able to renounce the childhood oath. Amazingly, she soon conceived and gave birth to a healthy, baby boy.[6] Of course, it is possible that the joyful conception wasn't related to the vows and certainly, the dramatic story doesn't imply that infertility is usually related to ungodly oaths. But the startling story triggered deeper thoughts about my own childhood vow.

After years of over-working in the ministry, I finally realized that something was wrong in my soul. I was unable to rest, and something kept me from deeply, truly enjoying time off. I was driven to do more and to do it better. Since there is no end to ministry, my workaholism was threatening my marriage.

One weekend, I decided to preach about the destructive power of inner vows. As I contemplated the Sandfords' dramatic story about the potentially binding effect of childhood oaths, I decided to put my own soul before the Lord. *God, I don't want to be a driven man, what's wrong with me?*

Rising out of my unconscious mind, I heard myself as a fourth grader, desperate for his dad to come back home, pledging: *I'll never rest until I have my family back together, happy and healthy again.* I suddenly realized that my childhood oath was the source of my grown-up attempt to be the perfect pastor.

But how? Mom and Dad were divorced and both re-married many years prior. There was no possibility of getting my family back together. How could that old vow still enslave me? That's when God spoke to the quietness of my heart.

> *Who's your family now, Alan?*
> *I have a wife and a baby, Lord.*
> *It's bigger than that. Who's your family now, Alan?*

I nodded my head and softly sobbed. *I know Lord, I know. The church is my extended family, isn't it? They're my brothers and sisters and mothers and fathers.* I began to replay the refrain: *I won't rest until I have my family back together, happy and healthy again.* Every person that left my church felt a little like Dad leaving again. Every church conflict felt like a threat to the well-being of my extended family. Though much of my work was born of love for people and passion to build God's kingdom, something else had been at work all along. I was fighting to keep my family together.

The answer for my marriage wasn't me trying to be a better, less-driven husband. The answer wasn't one more vow. The answer was to renounce a vow that I never should have made and never could keep. As soon as I said, "I'm not God. I can't make everyone happy and healthy, and I'm not going to try," the burden of drivenness lifted. A hidden tyrant was dethroned, and I was free to love my wife and family. Power to love your spouse doesn't come through making more religious vows – it more often comes through renouncing ungodly oaths.

For Further Reflection:

1) Paul says that the power of sin is the law. How are oaths like the law?
2) To begin an honest search to see if you have hidden, ungodly vows in your heart, take a few moments to acknowledge the wounds of your life. It's usually there, amidst life's pain, that we unconsciously make vows that we hope will protect us from further pain.

For Discussion Together:

1) If you think you are discerning an ungodly vow you've made, share it with your spouse.

2) Share with each other a promise of God from His Word that blesses and strengthens you.

Prayer for the Day:

Lord, thank You for the finished work of Jesus Christ. Teach us to truly rest in Christ's saving work. Put our whole attention upon Him. Grant us deeper vision of the sufficiency and decisiveness of His life, death, and resurrection. Keep our hearts from the strife-filled anxiety that accompanies unsure souls. Let no distraction or busyness of life ever pull us apart from one another or from You. Be exalted in us God. In Jesus' name, AMEN.

Week Three

Wednesday

The Folly of Ramping Up Our Oaths

"For while we were living in the flesh, our sinful passions, aroused by the law, were at work in our members to bear fruit for death. But now we are released from the law, having died to that which held us captive, so that we serve in the new way of the Spirit and not in the old way of the written code."

Romans 7:5-6

Knowing that you can't count on a person's ordinary "yes" or "no," we discovered as kids that you have to ramp up the commitment. Remember the scene that every kid who ever hung out in a tree fort, joined a secret club or just had a best buddy, has experienced?

Little Bobby: *"Can I tell you something that you won't tell anyone else?"*
Little Johnny: *"Yes."*
Little Bobby: *"Promise?"*
Little Johnny: *"I promise."*
Little Bobby: *"Do you swear?"*
Little Johnny: *"I swear."*
Little Bobby: *"Do you swear to God?"*
Little Johnny: *"I swear to God."*
Little Bobby: *"Do you swear to God, cross your heart, hope to die?"*
Little Johnny: *"Okay, I swear to God, cross my heart, hope to die."*

If you absolutely must get an honest answer from someone, we've learned that you have to ramp up the oath. The ascending oath scale moves from a simple "yes" or "no" to a promise. If "I promise" isn't enough, it moves to "I swear." If "I swear" isn't enough then you can resort to bringing God into the swearing. If getting God into the equation still isn't enough, you must add some serious curses or impending mortal danger likely to land upon the one who breaks the oath. We don't know any good way to get people to tell the truth or keep their promises. So we ramp up the seriousness of the oath.

Most appeals to Christian commitment aren't much more than ramped up oath-making. I heard a preacher on the radio recently teaching the Ephesians 5 scripture, "Husbands love your wives as Christ loved the church."

The radio preacher is a famous, popular minister. This was his message: "Husbands, you need to do more for your wives. Many of you aren't loving your wives the way Christ loved the church. You need to sacrifice for her more; you need to serve her more. You need to quit viewing your wife as a woman to clean your house and share your bed." The more he preached, the more angry I became.

Everything he said was true, it just wasn't helpful. The women listening to the radio that day were probably nodding their heads, gritting their teeth and thinking, *My husband ought to hear this.* I imagine the preacher ending his "challenging" sermon with an appeal for husbands to come forward and make a fresh commitment to be good husbands. *Will you come forward and commit yourself to loving your wife as Christ loved the church? Come on men. Make a commitment today.* And the men go forward, make new, heavier oaths than before and their wives wonder a few weeks later what went wrong.

Oaths to "try harder" to be a good husband or wife don't work because oaths are just like laws – they tell you what you must do lest you suffer the consequences. Oaths, like the law, never empower. In fact, Paul tells the Romans that our sinful passions are "aroused by the law." It runs contrary to intuition and to most of what you've heard from pulpits everywhere, but the path to becoming a better spouse isn't ramping up your vow to try harder. The true path is to revel in the finished work of Christ Jesus wherein you have been forgiven. The answer isn't swearing to God that you'll be better; the answer is God swearing to you through the cross of Christ.

For Further Reflection:

1) Spend time studying Romans 6 and 7.
2) Think about what Paul means when he contrasts the "new way of the Spirit" with the "old way of the written code." Reflect on or write down all that comes to mind that is better about life in the Spirit as opposed to life by the law.

For Discussion Together:

1) Can you remember a time as a child that you ramped up your oath?
2) As an adult, what have you been promising God that you'll do better?
3) Discuss an area of need in your lives or marriage. What promise of God applies to your area of need?

Prayer for the Day:
Lord, thank You that all Your promises are "yes and amen" in Christ. Great is Your faithfulness. Let Your Word dwell so richly in our hearts that our trust in You grows. Teach us how to live by Your glorious promises to us rather than our vows to You. Fill us with deep delight in the assurance of Your love for us and let that love spill out to others today. In Jesus' name, AMEN.

Week Three

Thursday

God Swears to God

"For when God made a promise to Abraham, since he had no one greater by whom to swear, he swore by himself...."

Hebrews 6:13

The story of Abraham, like the whole story of the Bible, is not, in the end, about Abraham's promises to God. It is about God's promises to Abraham. God was utterly committed to convincing Abraham that His promises were true.

In Genesis 12, God calls Abraham, blesses him and promises him a rich inheritance of land and descendants.

But in Genesis 15, God does more than speak with Abraham – God cuts a covenant. We refer to the process of establishing a covenant as "making" a covenant. But in the ancient Hebrew language, a covenant wasn't "made" it was "cut." This language makes sense when you understand the common, ancient practice by which representatives established covenants for their respective domains. If two kings or officials wanted to settle a matter via treaty, they would literally cut some animals in half and lay the bloodied carcasses in two parallel lines. As the leaders announced aloud their covenantal commitments, they would walk through the rows of sacrificed animals to symbolize the solemnity of their oaths. It was the ultimate "cross my heart and hope to die" vow. It was as if the covenant makers were saying, "May God make me like one of these slaughtered animals if I do not keep the promises that I make this day." The gravity of their oaths was pictured by the bloody sacrifices that surrounded them. They were swearing by God and swearing by the blood of the animals.

Though his call to be a father of a nation was fresh, Abraham had already begun to wonder whether God would uphold His promises. Would God really give him a son? "O Lord God, what will you give me, for I continue childless?" (Genesis 15:2).

That's when God did the unimaginable. He told Abraham to get a heifer, a goat, and a ram to slaughter in traditional covenant cutting practice. Abraham knew the drill. Cut the animals up and make the parallel lines of blood. *Soon, I'll be announcing my oaths and walking through these slain animals,* Abraham must have thought. Instead, "As the sun was going down, a deep sleep fell on Abram" (Genesis 15:12). In his sleeplike trance, Abraham couldn't move or speak. Instead, God moved. God spoke. "When the sun had gone down and it was dark, behold a smoking fire pot and a flaming torch passed between [the animal carcasses]" (Genesis 15:17). The fire symbolized God Himself. Abraham didn't walk through the bloody path, God did. Abraham didn't make an oath, God did. "On that day the Lord made a covenant with Abram, saying, 'To your offspring I give this land...'" (Genesis 15:18).

The power of the Christian's life doesn't come through your promises to God. The power of the Gospel comes through God's promises to you. God doesn't want your oaths to be a better spouse. He doesn't want your sacrifices and self-punishment. What does God want? He wants you to be sure of His grace. Know for certain that He will do as He has promised to do. Know for certain that He will never leave you. Know for certain that He has forgiven you. Know for certain that He loves you.

When God spoke to Abraham, it was as if God were saying, "If it is necessary to persuade you of my love, I will become like these bloodied, sacrificed animals."

And God did.

God became flesh. "Behold the Lamb of God" (John 1:29). The Lamb was slain. Slaughtered on a Roman cross on a hill outside Jerusalem. And there, while Jesus bled from his brow, his belly, his hands and feet, God made an oath.

To anyone who will receive Me – oh, to anyone who will believe in Me – I pledge you My love – I pledge you every spiritual blessing. I pledge you life abundant. I pledge you eternity in Heaven. I swear it to be true. I swear by ....

As God looked around the cosmos, there was no one great enough to swear by... no one but His Son hanging on a cross. So God cut a covenant in Jesus. God swore by God to love you forever.

For Further Reflection:

1) Read chapters 12 and 15 in Genesis.
2) Write down all the ways that the Lord spoke or acted to reassure Abraham of God's call on his life.

For Discussion Together:

1) Are there some areas in your life for which you need reassurance that God is with you? Share one with your spouse.
2) If God were to reassure you in your areas of insecurity and your uncertainties lifted, how would it bless your marriage?

Prayer for the Day:
Lord, You see our insecurities, and You know our needs. Whether through a whisper or a shout, speak Your loving reassurances into our hearts today. Build our faith by

granting us eyes to see You with us and in us. Free us of our anxieties by Your confidence-building presence. Amidst the uncertainties of life, let us know the certainty of Your great love for us in Jesus Christ. In His name we pray, AMEN.

Week Three

Friday

Breaking Oaths and Breaking Free

"I will visit you, and I will fulfill to you my promise and bring you back to this place. For I know the plans I have for you, declares the LORD, plans for welfare and not for evil, to give you a future and a hope. Then you will call upon me and come and pray to me, and I will hear you."

Jeremiah 29:10-12

In previous days, I shared how, as a ten-year-old boy, I made a vow that, no matter what, I wouldn't rest until I had my family back together, happy and healthy again. That vow silently drove me toward ministry workaholism and threatened my marriage. What's a grown man with a fourth grade wound to do with a soul-deep, life-long vow?

I renounced it.

I was the one who had made the law so I was entitled to revoke it. I asked the Lord to forgive me for making an ungodly, impossible oath that was driving me to perfectionism and exhaustion. And then, to really lay the axe to the roots of the vow, I decided to renounce it as boldly and publicly as I knew how.

I'll never forget that wonderful Sunday morning. In my sermon, I explained how inner oaths could develop from childhood wounds in our lives and how God gives us grace to replace those hidden tyrannical laws. Then came one of the most freeing moments I've ever experienced.

"I have a confession to make," I declared publicly. "Don't worry, I haven't had an affair." I heard the collective sigh of relief from the congregation. "When I was in the fourth grade, I made a vow that I would never rest until I had my family back together, happy and healthy again. Both of my parents remarried long ago. You are my family now. I've been working hard to keep you all together, happy and healthy. But I hereby repent of that foolish oath. The fact is, I can't control whether people stay together, happy and healthy. So from now on, I'm not going to try. I'm going to love you, and I'm going to preach the Gospel to you, and give you some of the tools of God's Word for the health of your souls. I hope you get along; that'd be just wonderful. But I can no longer make it my life's mission. I hereby renounce that childhood oath, in Jesus' name. I love you all, but my health and happiness will no longer depend on whether you're all together, happy and healthy. I hope it goes well for you, but that's up to you and God."

The people clapped. Maybe some angels clapped. I felt like God was smiling and putting His arm around me while I preached with maybe the lightest heart ever. And God smiled when I went home and rested, perhaps for the first time since fourth grade.

There's a light heart and rest for you, too.

Instead of vowing *I will do whatever it takes to have a good marriage*, listen to God's oath to you: "*I know the plans that I have for you, plans to prosper you and not to harm you, to give you a future and a hope*" (Jeremiah 29:11).

Instead of pledging, *I will not rest until I am fully accepted by my spouse*, hearken to God's voice: "*There is, therefore, now no condemnation for those who are in Christ Jesus*" (Romans 8:1).

Instead of making it your motto, *I will do whatever it takes to keep my spouse from leaving me,* receive God's promise: "*Never will I leave you; never will I forsake you*" (Hebrews 13:5).

You don't need to stand up in public and renounce your ill-gotten vows. It can be in the quiet of your home or over coffee with a friend or today in prayer with your spouse. Regardless of how or where, banish your ungodly oaths, and you can banish your fears. Banish your fears, and you'll be set free from your impatience, covetousness, and anger. In other words, if you want a more abundant marriage, don't swear to God that you'll try harder. God's sworn to God for you.

For Further Reflection:

1) Oaths, like all legalism, enslave us. Ask God to show you any unbiblical oaths in your heart.

2) If you have identified any oaths, confess them to God and renounce them. You can use words like: "I realize that I have made an oath never to let anyone hurt me. It's an impossible oath, and I renounce it as untrue and unbiblical."

3) Reflecting on God's Word, what are the truths that replace any unbiblical oaths you've discovered? For example, "It's impossible to keep people from ever hurting me. But, the glorious Gospel truth is that, even if I am hurt emotionally by others, God's acceptance of me in Christ will comfort and heal me. In Christ, I'll be okay, even if others hurt my feelings."

For Discussion Together:

1) Share with one another about any oaths you've uncovered.

2) Reaffirm truths from God's Word that replace the unbiblical oaths.

Alan D. Wright

Prayer for the Day:

Lord, continue to reveal to us any of the ways that we have developed our own legalistic oaths in an attempt to control our world. We acknowledge that You are the good and sovereign King over all creation. You alone are in control. You know our wounds and our insecurities. Meet us in the midst of old pain. Heal us. Transform us and teach us the way of grace that replaces the tyranny of inward vows. In Jesus' name we pray, AMEN.

Week Three

Saturday

Holding Each Other Accountable

"When God made his promise to Abraham, since there was no one greater for him to swear by, he swore by himself...."
Hebrews 6:13

If our oaths to try harder to be good spouses don't work, we often think that what we need is more accountability. *If I'm going to get victory over my struggle with lust, I'll need a serious Christian like Joe to be my accountability partner.* So Joe agrees to keep the sinner accountable. I'm not making light of the sin of lust, but the whole accountability drill can become comical.

Joe: *I'll meet you every week at 6 am on Friday morning to see how you're doing.*
Sinner: *Okay, sounds great. Thanks so much, Joe.*
Joe (at 6 am Friday morning): *Sinner, how are you?*
Sinner: *I'm good.*
Joe: *Be honest with me. Did you lust this week?*
Sinner: *I can't lie. I did lust but not until Tuesday.*
Joe: *I'm going to have to meet with you earlier next Friday so we have more time. Let's make it 5 am for good measure. Can you get up and be here at 5 am? Do you promise not to lust this week?*
Sinner: *I promise. I'll meet you next Friday at 5 am. It'll be a lust-free week, I promise.*
Joe (at 5 am the following Friday): *Look me in the eye – you did it, didn't you? You lusted again this week, didn't you?*
Sinner: *Yes, but I made it to Wednesday!*
Joe*: I guess I'm going to have to start meeting with you two days a week.*

I make light of the ramped-up accountability not because I don't see value in having such friends but because we go about it exactly backwards. We need accountability partners to help us in our marriages but not for the purpose of reminding us what sinners we are. We need accountability to remember the Good News. We need to be reminded who we are in Christ and what we were made for. We need accountability partners who bless us in the name of Jesus. Christian accountability is not helping one another make more oaths to keep more laws!

Attempting to grow by being held accountable to the law can't be God's plan because of one, irrefutable reason: it is a formula for fear. Any system that induces fear can't be God's system because the Lord has declared hundreds of times in His Word, "Do not be afraid." The success of accountability under the system of the law depends upon fear of negative consequences to the sinner. In order to increase the commitment, the consequences must become increasingly ominous. People will try harder to be good if they are afraid of the consequences for being bad, but the effort seldom lasts and the energy derived from fear wreaks havoc. Why would God tell you 365 times in His Word to "fear not" if His plan for your sanctification requires continued fear of condemnation? God has given you His Word, put His Son on the cross and poured out His Holy Spirit upon you not so that you will worry about the stability of His love but so that you will become convinced of His love. We are not sanctified by finding an accountability partner who holds us to the law. We are sanctified by accountability partners who remind us of the Gospel, how accepted we are in the Beloved and our great destiny in Christ.

For Further Reflection:

1) Make an honest list of your fears.
2) How would a deeper experience of the perfect love of God dissolve those fears?

For Discussion Together:

1) What sorts of Christian accountability have you had in the past? Share what was helpful and what wasn't helpful.
2) Christian accountability isn't so much reminding one another of what sinners we are. It is more a process of reminding one another of what God has done for us and who we are in Christ. With this view in mind, share with your spouse at least one reminder of who she/he is in Christ.

Prayer for the Day:
Father, reveal to us the depths of Your love and acceptance of us in Christ. Teach us how to encourage one another with the glory of the Gospel. May we hold each other accountable, not reminding one another of our failings, but reminding one another of our position as Your children and as co-heirs with Christ. In Jesus' name, AMEN.

WEEK FOUR

Accepting a New Identity

Week Four

Sunday

Loving Your Spouse as You Love Yourself

"And one of the scribes came up and heard them disputing with one another, and seeing that he answered them well, asked him 'Which commandment is the most important of all?' Jesus answered, 'The most important is, "Hear, O Israel: The Lord our God, the Lord is one. And you shall love the Lord your God with all your heart and with all your soul and with all your mind and with all your strength." The second is this: "You shall love your neighbor as yourself." There is no other commandment greater than these.' And the scribe said to him, 'You are right, Teacher. You have truly said that he is one, and there is no other besides him.'"

Mark 12:28–32

Priceless parental moments come as surprises. You can't plan for the breakthrough conversations you have with your kids. You can't predict when a tender or teachable moment will pop up. They just happen and, later you think, *Wow, I'll never forget that.*

Bennett was ten years old. We were on the way to the golf course when he brought up, of all things, the subject of addiction. "Dad, how can you get addicted to something?"

"Well, umm," I swallowed hard, "Bennett, if you're addicted to something, you feel like you have to have it and if you don't have it you start really wanting it. Addictions are awful because they take control of your life and the things you are addicted to usually end up hurting you. Why do you ask?"

"I saw on ESPN something about a professional golfer who blew two million dollars gambling. They said he had a gambling addiction. Can you be addicted to gambling?"

"Yes, Bennett, you can be addicted to gambling. You can be addicted to a lot of things." I half chuckled as I muttered under my breath, *"You can be addicted to golf!"*

After a few moments, our priceless conversation continued with a further query: "Dad, why would he become addicted to gambling? I don't understand. He's one of the best golfers in the world. He is famous. He is rich. He gets to play golf all the time and gets paid to do commercials. He has just about the perfect life. Why would he get addicted to something like gambling?"

Wow. How do I formulate a ten-year-old's version

of all that I've learned about the deep, complex sources of addiction? How can I explain how childhood wounds, innate sin and deep-seated shame become the breeding ground of chemical, emotional and psychological dependencies? How can I explain to a pre-adolescent how a deep sense of inadequacy in the unaffirmed soul creates a gnawing anxiety? How can I describe the pain of an anxious psyche that is beleaguered by the angst of feeling unloved? How can I portray the process by which the restless heart looks for a means to mask the inward anxiety? Do I explain that drugs temporarily release happy feelings in the brain but that gambling or pornography or chocolate also activate natural, hormonal chemicals in the brain that temporarily make people feel less fearful? I opted for the simplest terms I know.

"Bennett, as strange as it may sound, that professional golfer isn't happy with himself, and he's looking for something to make him happy. Even though he's made a lot of money and he's famous and gets to play golf all the time, deep down, he doesn't feel good about himself."

It was quiet for a long moment. Then, my ten-year-old boy blurted out the words I would have most wanted to hear but never would have predicted:

"Well," Bennett spoke with confidence and a slow, happy drawl, "I lo-o-ve myself."

After I muffled my laughter and silently thanked God, I simply responded, "Good, Bennett. As long as you love yourself you'll probably never be addicted to anything."

If you want to love your spouse, you're going to first have to love yourself.

For Further Reflection:

1) Read today's Scripture again (Mark 12:28-32).
2) How is "loving yourself" linked to "loving your neighbor"?
3) Is "loving yourself" a form of selfishness or something different?

For Discussion Together:

1) Think together about the words of author and counselor Leeanne Payne: *"If we are busy hating the soul that God loves and is in the process of straightening out, we cannot help others – our minds will be riveted on ourselves – not on Christ who is our wholeness. When we hate the self, ... we are self-conscious rather than God-conscious."[7]*
2) Discuss the idea of "loving yourself." Does it seem like a foreign concept to you or something that already comes naturally?
3) Share with your spouse at least one way that you struggle to love yourself.

Prayer for the Day:
Lord God, You have loved us with an everlasting love. You have set Your affection upon us, died for us and adopted us as Your own. Show us today any of the ways that we do

not love ourselves. Teach us the difference between selfishness and self-love. Grant us grace to overcome the temptation toward self-condemnation and fill us today with love in Christ for one another and for ourselves. In Jesus' name, AMEN.

Week Four

Monday

Rejecting Self-Rejection

"Having predestined us unto the adoption of children by Jesus Christ to himself, according to the good pleasure of his will, To the praise of the glory of his grace, wherein he hath made us accepted in the beloved."

Ephesians 1:5-6, KJV

As part of their premarital counseling, I ask most prospective grooms to read Charlie Shedd's classic little book, *Letters to Philip.* The collection of letters conveys a father's timeless advice to his son about how to treat a woman. I want engaged men to read it for many reasons, not the least of which is, if they begin reading the

145

book, they will surely make it to chapter two. The second chapter of *Letters to Philip* can change everything about the way a husband understands the power invested in him. Pastor Shedd tells Philip about a day that a young woman named Frances met him at his minister's study. Knowing how Charlie loved to hear success stories, the attractive, confident wife wanted to share with her pastor why she thought her mate, Mark, was the best husband in the world.

"From the day I started school" [Frances began], "clear up to college, everyone made fun of my legs. As you can see, they look like tree stumps."

When she voluntarily stood up to display them, Pastor Shedd saw that, yes, they did look like tree stumps. But, at the same time, he was amazed that she didn't seem embarrassed in the least by this unusual bodily feature.

"Sometimes when I was little I would cry myself to sleep.... In high school I dated some but never more than a couple of times with any one boy and you can guess why...."

Frances soon shared how she had met Mark in college and how much she liked him right away. Though Mark never once commented about her legs, she often did. "You know, looking for assurance," she told the pastor.

One night, Mark took Frances' hands, looked her in the eye and spoke clearly: "Frances, I want you to quit knocking yourself. I love you the way you are. The Lord gave you good, sturdy legs. They give me a solid feeling and I like it." Frances just cried.

Sometime later, Mark took Frances home to meet his mother. Frances nearly melted when she saw her boy-friend's mom. She had a disability in one of her legs. She wore a built up shoe and walked with a big limp.

Here's what Frances told Pastor Shedd about that moment with her boyfriend: "I looked at him and he looked at me and I think I loved him right then like nobody ever loved a man before... that was thirteen years ago and now I can honestly laugh about my legs. Can you see why I say he's wonderful? There isn't one thing in the world I wouldn't do for Mark!"[8]

Until that marvelous moment, Mark loved Frances, but Frances didn't love herself. Their relationship would never be abundant until Frances accepted herself. The block in the relationship wasn't Mark's rejection of Frances, it was Frances' rejection of herself. If we don't believe ourselves accepted, we remain afraid. When we are afraid it makes us insecure. It's often our insecurities that trouble our marriages the most. It was only when Frances accepted herself that her fear was banished. Maybe the greatest gift you could give your spouse is accepting yourself.

As with Frances, the only real way to accept yourself is to experience acceptance from another. Through Christ, you were "accepted in the beloved" forever. If the Lord of the universe has accepted you, you might as well accept yourself.

For Further Reflection:

1) Read Ephesians 1:1-14.
2) Underline or write down the phrases and statements that emphasize how accepted you are in Christ.
3) Take an honest self-inventory by comparing your view of yourself with God's view of your position in Christ according to Ephesians 1.

For Discussion Together:

1) Have there been times when you have seen your spouse rejecting him/herself? If so, share some helpful, healing words. You might use words like: "Sometimes you put yourself down by saying _____, but I want you to know that God accepts you and I accept you."
2) Read Ephesians 1:3-14 to your spouse, making it personal. ("... who has blessed <u>you</u> with every spiritual blessing... has chosen <u>you</u> in Christ....")

Prayer for the Day:
Lord, thank You that You have blessed us with every spiritual blessing in Christ. You have chosen us in Christ and declared us holy and blameless by the shed blood of Christ.

Oh God, let us not reject that which You have already accepted. Let us not condemn that which You have declared righteous. Fill us today with fresh assurances that we have been accepted in the Beloved. Empower us to accept ourselves in Christ. It is in His name we pray, AMEN.

WEEK FOUR

TUESDAY

The Difference Between Self-Love and Self-Absorption

"Not long after that, the younger son got together all he had, set off for a distant country and there squandered his wealth in wild living. After he had spent everything, there was a severe famine in that whole country, and he began to be in need. So he went and hired himself out to a citizen of that country, who sent him to his fields to feed pigs. He longed to fill his stomach with the pods that the pigs were eating, but no one gave him anything."

Luke 15:13-16

The "Parable of the Prodigal Son" tells about a boy who insulted his dad, ran away from home, squandered his inheritance in gross sin, and shamed his family name.

See there, we may be quick to assert. *There is a picture of a man in love with himself. That younger son only cared about himself. That's the problem with the world today, too. Young people love themselves and nobody else. And that's the problem with marriages. People are so in love with themselves that they don't have time to love their spouses.*

Loved himself? Really? Think about it.

Think of a person you love. Perhaps it's your son or daughter. Maybe you envision a husband or wife or a best friend. Would you ever, in your wildest imagination, on your worst day, do to the one you love what the younger brother did to himself? Would you ever lead someone you love into abject rebellion? Would you ever counsel someone you love into rejection of the blessings of home, heritage and family? Would you ever curse someone you love with the folly of wasteful living? Would you ever relegate someone you love to the prostitutes and pigpens?

Of course not. You would only do those things to someone you hated.

Love never makes us want to hurt someone. That's what hate does. When you have hate in your heart toward someone, you secretly want him to suffer. When you hate someone, you want the worst for her.

The younger son greedily grabbed his inheritance, wasted it foolishly, sinned recklessly, and fell into ruin because inwardly he deeply disdained his life.

When you consider the harmful things you do to yourself – subjecting your mind to unedifying things, neglecting your health, abusing substances, working too much, demanding personal perfection, putting yourself down – how can you call that love? It might be one of the most sobering questions you've ever considered, but would you ever treat someone you love the way you treat yourself?

The younger son's problem was not self-love it was self-absorption. Narcissism is not a personality disorder describing those who love themselves but those who are consumed with themselves. Like the mythical figure, Narcissus, who fell in love with his image reflecting in the water, self-consumed souls are obsessed with their image precisely because they are discontent with themselves. When we accept ourselves we don't need to think about ourselves all the time. When we are constantly considering our image, worrying and wondering what others think of us, we can be sure that we do not love ourselves unconditionally. We can never love our mates if we are absorbed with ourselves, and we will be forever absorbed with ourselves until we love ourselves through Christ.

For Further Reflection:

1) Read the parable of the two sons in Luke 15:11-32.

2) Think about some of your own self-destructive behaviors. How would loving yourself change the way you feel about those behaviors?

3) Be honest with yourself. In what ways are you absorbed with yourself? How would truly loving yourself change your self-absorption?

For Discussion Together:

1) Are you more like the older son or the younger son? Share your responses and reflections with one another.

2) Choose one way to fill in the blank and share it with your spouse. "I struggle to love myself in this way _____."

Prayer for the Day:
Lord, teach us the difference between self-absorption and self-love. Grant us eyes to see ourselves through the lens of Christ, His cross and His resurrection. Expose any self-hatred that triggers our self-destructive behaviors. Keep us from maligning that which You have blessed and called good. Fill our hearts with a deep willingness to receive Your love and to embrace the destiny You give us. You have redeemed our lives in Christ, and we trust that you have something good in store for us today. In Jesus' name, AMEN.

WEEK FOUR

WEDNESDAY

Escaping the Two Opposite Paths of Self-Absorption

"Now his older son was in the field, and as he came and drew near to the house, he heard music and dancing. And he called one of the servants and asked what these things meant. And he said to him, 'Your brother has come, and your father has killed the fattened calf, because he has received him back safe and sound.' But he was angry and refused to go in. His father came out and entreated him, but he answered his father, 'Look, these many years I have served you, and I never disobeyed your command, yet you never gave me a young goat, that I might celebrate with my friends. But when this son of yours came, who has devoured your property with prostitutes, you killed the fattened calf for him!'"

Luke 15:25-30

The urgent need to accept yourself in Christ isn't for your benefit alone; it is vital for the sake of your spouse as well. Only when you accept your Heavenly Father's love can you truly accept yourself. Only when you accept yourself, can you accept your spouse. The unaffirmed self cannot affirm another.

The parable of the two sons masterfully portrays the path and pitfalls of self-absorption. Only one son accepts the father's love and thus accepts himself. The son who never accepts the father's love can never accept himself. He is relegated to a mentality of slavery rather than sonship. Clearly, the son who does not accept himself cannot enjoy real relationship. True, intimate marriage emerges when both husband and wife let go of self-absorption in order to share their lives. The way out of self-absorption is, ironically, self-acceptance.

While the younger brother in Jesus' parable expressed self-contempt through rebellion, the older brother was at home punishing himself in a different way. The older brother rejected himself through slavish self-righteousness. When the festive welcome-home party erupted upon the return of the younger son, the older brother was still working in the field. He heard the music and the dancing, but the "older brother became angry and refused to go in. So his father went out and pleaded with him. But he answered his father, 'Look! All these years I've been slaving for you and never disobeyed your orders'" (Luke 15:28-29).

Both boys made the same hellish false assumption about life in their father's house. They both assumed that they were under the law. The younger brother responded to the law by rebelling. *No one is going to tell me what to do.* The older brother responded to the law by trying to keep it perfectly. It's not clear which poison, rebellious abandonment of the father or religious manipulation of the father, is more destructive. Though the younger brother sins in a far off land, the older brother at home may be the more distant one. Both the younger, in his self-absorbed wild life, and the older, in his perfectionistic driven life, are narcissistically selfish. Though one son wastes his money on pleasures and the other son labors to impress his dad, both sons are self-absorbed. Society applauds people like the older son who are committed to proper appearances. But Jesus does not applaud the dutiful first born. In fact, the great lament of the story is over the elder brother's absence from the celebration.

"'My son,' the father said, 'you are always with me, and everything I have is yours. But we had to celebrate...'" (Luke 15:31). *Please, son, please. Please come into the party.*

While the younger son punishes himself with his promiscuity, the older son punishes himself with his perfectionism. The path to intimacy in marriage requires deep, self-acceptance in Christ. If we are self-absorbed like the younger son, we have no time to love our mates because we are consumed with masking our angst via rebellion. If we are self-absorbed like the older son, we have no time to love our mates because we are too busy pursuing per-fection. The way to intimacy is the way of self-acceptance through the grace of Christ Jesus.

For Further Reflection:

1) Read the story of the two sons again.
2) What drew the younger son home? What kept the older son away from the celebration?

For Discussion Together:

1) Are you more likely to punish yourself with rebel-lion or perfectionism? Discuss your answers.
2) Is there anything keeping you from experiencing the Father's embrace?

Prayer for the Day:
Lord, we want to be in Your arms. Show us any ways that we are robbing ourselves of the grace You so freely offer us. Draw us in from the far away place of the younger son and from the nearby field of the older son. Keep us from the self-absorption of rebellion and the self-absorption of religion. Shower us and shield us with Your immeasurable grace today. In Jesus' name, AMEN.

Week Four

Thursday

Accepting Yourself in Christ

"But when he came to himself, he said, 'How many of my father's hired servants have more than enough bread, but I perish here with hunger! I will arise and go to my father, and I will say to him, "Father, I have sinned against heaven and before you. I am no longer worthy to be called your son. Treat me as one of your hired servants."' And he arose and came to his father. But while he was still a long way off, his father saw him and felt compassion, and ran and embraced him and kissed him."

Luke 15:17-20

The younger son's process of self-acceptance did not begin until "he came to his senses" (Luke 15:17). Realizing that his father's servants were well fed, he exclaimed to himself, "Here I am starving to death! I will set out and go back..." (vss. 17-18, NIV). In his contrition and repentance, the younger son was revealing the beginning steps of self-acceptance: *I have failed. I have scandalized the family. I am unworthy. But my life is not over. I can go back. I can start over. I do not condemn myself to a pigpen prison for the rest of my life. I will be honest with my father about my failures and my unworthiness, and perhaps he will accept me anyway.*

Self-acceptance is born from another's acceptance. We can only accept ourselves when someone we trust demonstrates to us that we are acceptable. The younger son's risky move toward his father was not a manipulative, religious stunt. The son was, probably for the first time in his life, able to really be himself. There was greater joy in the simple freedom of being real with his dad, than in all the parties, promiscuity, and popularity combined. Oh, the sweet, delicious freedom of finally being yourself. *Here I am father. Broken, humiliated, hungry and needing to be held.*

It wasn't the robe, the ring, the sandals and fattened calf that changed the child. It was the father's heart. It was a daddy accepting his boy. The boy left home wanting to assert his independence and prove that he was all grown up. But it wasn't until he was weeping in his father's arms that the boy became a man. In the end, it wasn't a complicated, mystical self-realization that the boy needed.

He needed identification with his father. Contrary to the popular self-esteem movements of recent decades, the path to self-acceptance is not found within ourselves. If you look within yourself in order to accept yourself, you'll despair when you see your sins and your failures. The wayward son didn't look within himself and find an inward holiness that boosted his self-esteem. Instead, the boy found his worth in his father's embrace.

The younger brother had rehearsed his soliloquy of repentance, but the lavish father interrupted his son's speech and began the celebration. As scandalous as it seems, there was no demand for penance, no required religious gestures, and no repayment requested. For the first time since the foolish son had started his riotous living, the boy was no longer absorbed with himself. Suddenly, his life wasn't about his own image. When deeply embraced by the Father, sons and daughters have no need to ask the questions that plague most souls: *What do people think of me? Am I popular? Do I look successful? Am I happy?* Suddenly, his life was rooted in his father's affection. *I belong to him. I belong here. I am loved by my father. I matter. I am accepted.*

A husband and wife discover one another's arms of love only to the extent they have been in the Father's arms of love. There in His arms, accepted by God in Jesus Christ, we finally can be set free from our self-absorption as we accept ourselves. There, in His embrace, we learn how to truly embrace our mates.

For Further Reflection:

1) Compare and contrast the younger son with the older son in Luke 15. Pay special attention to the younger son's response to the father's love and the older son's response to the father's pleadings.

2) How do you imagine the younger son's experience of the father's love changed him?

For Discussion Together:

1) Was there ever a time when you expected someone to condemn you but the person accepted you and forgave you? How did it impact you?

2) Have you ever had a moment like the younger son when you "came to your senses" and returned to God? Share it with your spouse.

Prayer for the Day:
Father, thank You for forgiving us through the shed blood of Jesus. Thank You for running to us with Your grace when we deserved only condemnation. Thank You for welcoming us, accepting us, and celebrating us in Christ. Keep us near Your heart. Keep us in Your embrace. Guard us from our selfish ways by convincing us that we are free in Christ. Whisper assurances of our inheritance to us by Your Spirit.

Convince us of Your mercies and make us trophies of Your grace. In Jesus' name, AMEN.

WEEK FOUR

FRIDAY

Eliminating Self-Sabotage

*"I know how to be brought low, and I know how to abound.
In any and every circumstance, I have learned the secret of
facing plenty and hunger, abundance and need. I can do all
things through him who strengthens me."*

Philippians 4:12-13

I played tennis as a kid. I loved the game and played it almost every day of my growing up years. Playing on the junior tennis circuit, I learned who had a good serve, who had a weak backhand, and who made dishonest calls. But the main thing I learned was whether they were ranked ahead of me, which usually meant they were seeded ahead of me in the tournament. It was ridiculous, but I figured that the rankings gave me enough information to determine whether I could beat someone or not. I always knew where I stood. If I was ranked higher than my opponent, I felt a bit nervous because I was supposed to win. But I would usually overcome my nerves and win. If I was ranked lower than my opponent, I would play hard, but deep inside I had already rehearsed the probable failure, and I almost always lost. It sounds silly and simplistic, but if you tell yourself that you'll probably fail, in order to prove that you're not a liar, you'll find a way to fail. If you tell yourself that your marriage will never get better, you'll probably find a way to keep your marriage in trouble.

That was my tennis mindset until I started focusing on playing doubles with Andy Grolnick. I was a short, quick kid, and Andy was a tall, lanky kid. We were a strange sight but a good blend of talent. Andy had a powerful serve and overhead smash while I had a quick step to cover the court and a consistent topspin forehand. I needed Andy's height and power, but the thing I needed most from Andy was his crazy thinking. He was a super-intelligent kid with academic prowess, but sometimes I thought Andy was too naive to recognize who was better than us.

"Andy, do you know who we play this week? These guys are ranked second in the state."

"So what? Big deal. We can beat them. They're no better than us."

"'But Andy, they're ranked second. You really think we can beat them?"

"Of course we can."

We won a lot of matches not because I believed we could win, but because I believed that Andy believed that we could. For the first time in my tennis career, I quit assuming I would lose to higher ranked players. I started becoming as crazy as Andy thinking that we could beat almost anybody. By year end, we had won the North Carolina Eastern Regional, and we were the number one seed in the state high school tournament.

If I could sabotage myself in something as trivial as tennis, what about all the important arenas of life? How many other ways do I unconsciously defeat myself? Ever wonder why so many of our mistakes are recurring errors? A couple finally gets their finances in order and then makes another bad investment. Why do they continuously make poor financial decisions? They're keeping their rank. A husband tries to be more patient but keeps losing his cool. Why? It might be self-sabotage. A woman loses weight only to regain it. What's needed to break the cycle? Maybe it's a new identity in Christ. At some point, you need an Andy Grolnick to plant the crazy thought: *maybe I can play at a higher level.* At some point you need to hear God tell you who you are in Christ so you can take the limits off your life and off your marriage.

For Further Reflection:

1) Spend some time reading the opening chapter of Ephesians.
2) Write down at least five characteristics of your new identity in Christ.

For Discussion Together:

1) Have you ever had an Andy Grolnick in your life? Share about a person who helped you take the limits off your life.
2) Have you noticed any habits of self-sabotage in your life? Share with your spouse.

Prayer for the Day:
Lord, life has enough challenges without us sabotaging ourselves. We don't want to reject Your call or decline Your blessing. Set us free from all patterns of small thinking. Expose our self-limiting ways and grant us fresh vision – Your vision – for our lives. Today, when we face a challenge, let us see ourselves positioned in Christ. Be exalted in our hearts and in our lives, Oh Lord. Grant us grace today that assures us we can do all things through Christ Jesus, in whose name we pray, AMEN.

Week Four

Saturday

Meet Your Maker

"But this is what was uttered through the prophet Joel: 'And in the last days it shall be, God declares, that I will pour out my Spirit on all flesh... before the day of the Lord comes, the great and magnificent day..'"

Acts 2:16,17,20

Christians and non-Christians have this in common: neither wants to think about the day they meet their maker. However, strange as it seems, one of the best things you could do for your marriage is to think more about Judgment Day. I preached a series on the subject recently. You can imagine how the crowd responded the Sunday when I announced that I planned to preach for five weeks on the subject. Can you hear the muffled groan? Sort of an "ooooh" with no "ahhhh."

I called the series "Meet Your Maker" because the title is laden with irony.[9] On the one hand, if you really want to threaten someone with doom, you say (with a Clint Eastwood expression on your face): "Get ready to meet your maker." On the other hand, it should be the greatest delight and most hopeful expectation of the Christian's heart to actually meet his maker.

To understand Judgment Day, a good starting place is the often-repeated biblical notion of "The Day of the Lord."[10] The "Day of the Lord" references have at least three features in common: 1) It's a decisive day in which evil is judged, God is exalted and the world is never the same again; 2) Something wonderful happens for the people of God; 3) It is accompanied by strange imagery of fire, wind and shaking. Most people think of The Day of the Lord (or Judgment Day) as a single day in the future that occurs at the end of the world. It's true, there is a future Day of the Lord, a final Judgment Day. But here is astonishing news that should make a Christian shout for joy from every available mountaintop: the Day of the Lord has already come, evil has already been judged, and we've already been declared righteous!

In Acts 2, on the day of Pentecost (the summer festival for Israel) the Holy Spirit came like a rushing wind. Images of fire, like tongues, rested on the believers and the whole place shook with the glory of God's grace. When

Peter stood up to preach the first Christian sermon, he said: "*For these people are not drunk, as you suppose, since it is only the third hour of the day. But this is what was uttered through the prophet Joel: 'And in the last days it shall be, God declares, that I will pour out my Spirit on all flesh, and your sons and your daughters shall prophesy, and your young men shall see visions, and your old men shall dream dreams...*'" (Acts 2:15–17).

He proceeded to quote the entire Joel prophecy of The Day of the Lord, "*the sun shall be turned to darkness and the moon to blood, before the day of the Lord comes, the great and magnificent day*" (Acts 2:20).

In other words, Peter announced a wonderful, preposterous, glorious truth: the Day of the Lord had arrived. It's hard to believe, but the first Christian sermon was about Judgment Day!

Why would thinking about Judgment Day help your marriage? Because there is no greater news than the assurance that the cross of Jesus Christ was decisive and that the resurrection was victorious over evil. There is no greater news than Judgment Day because it means that through simple faith in the Son of God, you and your spouse have already been judged in Christ and found not guilty. It means that because you are not condemned, you don't need to condemn one another. It means that you can come near God today, and you can be filled with God's Spirit every day.

There is a Day of the Lord at the final coming of Christ, but the wind and the fire and the shaking have already come just like Joel foresaw. Let the wind of the Spirit blow in and through your marriage! Let the fire of God's glorious grace rest upon your relationship to proclaim His goodness across the globe. Let the old ways of religious legalism be shaken to the very foundation and reassembled in mercy! May the grace of God be multiplied in your marriage!

For Further Reflection:

1) According to Rabbinical tradition, the first Pentecost took place at Mt. Sinai when God gave Moses the law. Read Exodus 19 for the account.
2) Compare Exodus 19 (the first Pentecost according to tradition) with the Pentecost story of Acts 2. What similar images do you notice? What are the big differences?

For Discussion Together:

1) Do you ever think about Judgment Day? In the past, as you've considered Judgment Day, did it make your feel hopeful or worried? Explain.
2) Most couples seldom talk about death. Take a few moments to share what you're most looking forward to when you think about going to Heaven.

Prayer for the Day:

Lord, we praise You that in Christ Jesus we have already been declared not guilty. Take away our fears of death and judgment. Fill us with the sure and certain hope of resurrection and life everlasting. Fill us with fresh confidence in the finished work of Jesus. Reassure us of Your love by granting us new vision of the Heavenly courtroom in which you handed down judgment against evil and doled out pardon and blessing to us. Silence the voice of the Accuser. Let the wind of the Spirit blow in us. Let the fire of Your love rest upon us. Let your grace shake away every vestige of legalistic religion in us so that we are free to love one another as You have loved us. Grant us a taste of Pentecost again today. In Jesus' name we pray, AMEN.

END NOTES

1. Gene Hill, "As Was the Father, So Is the Son", *Seasons of the Angler: A Fisherman's Anthology*, p.143 ed., David Seybold and illustrated by Joseph Fornelli, April 1, 1998.

2. F. B. Meyer, *Our Daily Walk*, May 7 (Grand Rapids: Zondervan, 1951). Accessed 2-28-2012 at http://www.preceptaustin.org/our_daily_walk_by_f_b_meyer_-_may.htm

3. Leanne Payne, *Restoring the Christian Soul: Overcoming Barriers to Completion in Christ through Healing Prayer* [Paperback] (Grand Rapids: Baker Books, March 1, 1996), 85.

4. Wayne Grudem, (2009-05-11). *Systematic Theology: An Introduction to Biblical Doctrine* (p. 726). Zondervan. Kindle Edition.

5. Online story, February, 2009 http://www.cbsnews.com/2100-500159_162-1762234.html

6. John and Paula Sandford, *Transformation of the Inner Man* (Tulsa, OK: Victory House, 1982), 191-192.

7. *Restoring the Christian Soul,* 32-33.

8. Charlie W. Shedd, *Letters to Philip* (New York: Jove Book/ Doubleday, 1978), 17- 18.

9. The idea for the series title was taken from a lyric from internationally acclaimed folk rock band Mumford and Sons. "In these bodies we will live, in these bodies we will die/ And where you invest your love, you invest your life./Awake my soul.../For you were made to meet your maker." Upon hearing the song, I thought, *of course, the invitation to meet your maker isn't a threat – it's what we were made for!*

10. For example, see Malachi 4:5-6; Zechariah 14:7-9; Zephaniah 1:7-9; and Joel 2:28-32.

For other resources, free audio downloads, radio broadcast stations or more information about Alan Wright's conference ministry, visit www.sharingthelight.org.

About Alan Wright's other books:

Free Yourself, Be Yourself: Find the Power to Escape Your Past

Isn't it time you shed performance-based living? Shame is a lie that whispers: *You don't measure up, and you need to make yourself acceptable if you're ever going to be loved.* But the Gospel announces a message just the opposite: *You can't make yourself acceptable but God already has in Jesus Christ!* Discover freedom through the power of the Gospel, and get the shame off you for good.

"This book will set thousands free from a shame they did not even know was suffocating them."

Dudley Hall, Author, Speaker, and President of Kerygma Ventures

A Childlike Heart: Recapture the Freedom of a Child

Ever longed for the days when life was slower and simpler? Remember how you wished the long summer days wouldn't end, when meals and naps were unwelcome intruders? What happened on the path to adulthood that made dinner and bed the highlights of the day? If you've ever longed to be like a child again, you can! Jesus said so. Rekindle the joy of your walk with God as you delve deep into Jesus' metaphor of childlike faith.

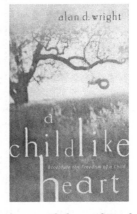

"I love this book.... Alan D. Wright has a gift for making happy memories come alive."

Barbara Johnson, best-selling author of *Stick a Geranium in Your Hat and Be Happy*

Lover of My Soul: Delighting in God's Passionate Love

God's Love. You've heard about it with your ears. You've believed it in your mind. Now, experience it in your heart. In this captivating portrait of God's love, discover how much Jesus cares for you, how He wants to provide for you and how much He desires to hold you close to Himself. Revel in His love. After all, it's a match made in Heaven.

"The incredible reality that God pursues us in love comes to life in *Lover of My Soul*. Ancient biblical accounts explode in the heart as Alan Wright uses contemporary idioms to bring home the intimate nature of our relationship with God."

Gary D. Chapman, best-selling author
of *The Five Love Languages*

God Moments: Recognizing and Remembering God's Presence in Your Life

Looking back, you see it: He was there. He moved. Your life changed ... *in a moment*. Join a joyful treasure hunt to uncover the *God Moments* within your own life history – even if you didn't recognize them as they happened. Discover more of God in your past, and you'll find more faith for today. Forget not all His benefits because the way you remember yesterday determines how you will face tomorrow!

"This is a great book that will change the way you see your past, change the way you see God, and help you see your life through new eyes."

Dr. Steve Stephens,
Psychologist,
author and radio host

CPSIA information can be obtained
at www.ICGtesting.com
Printed in the USA
FFOW05n2017201214